JustDickingAbout presents

HUMANITY BREEDS PROFANITY

RANDOM THOUGHTS AGAINST MY BETTER JUDGMENT

WRITTEN BY STEVE WYATT
TYPE DESIGN BY THE HAYES BROS

STEVE WYATT

Steve Wyatt is a writer and Creative Director who is still happily married to his first (and only) beautiful and talented wife. However, she is not so happily married, especially when Steve pretended to have a second wife on the back cover just because he thought it was an amusing way to mention that this is his second book. That was disrespectful and he regrets his decision to belittle the love and devotion he has for his first (and only) beautiful and talented wife. He would also like to thank his beautiful and talented wife for writing this clarifying statement and for compassionately listening when he requested,
"Not the face! Not the face!"

THE HAYES BROS

The Hayes Brothers are so damn talented, they have no idea why they're still associating with the likes of Steve. Since the last book was released, they have won numerous film awards and dedicated many hours to making sure they remain identical twins. If one goes for a run, the other has to go for a run, because who wants to be referred to as "the fatter one." To tell them apart, Adam is on the right and Nick is on the left. They recently switched sides to see what the world looks like from each other's perspective because they're always pushing creative boundaries like that.
Visit HayesHayes.com to see their multifaceted skill set.
It makes Steve sick.

© 2021 by Steve Wyatt. All rights reserved.

ISBN 978-0-578-84827-3

SHAMELESS PROMOTION

MY FIRST BOOK IS STILL AVAILABLE ON AMAZON.COM AND AMAZON.CO.UK.

IT WAS ONCE RANKED AT #31,665 ON AMAZON'S
BEST-SELLERS LIST FOR HUMOR BOOKS.
THEN SOMEBODY BOUGHT ONE AND IT JUMPED TO #1,276.
(HOW'S THAT FOR A FUCKED-UP ALGORITHM?)

(THE BOOK'S COVER IS ACTUALLY BRIGHT YELLOW, LIKE FRESH SNOW IN A CITY DOG RUN.)

IF YOU FIND PAGE NUMBERS USEFUL, I'VE COLLATED THEM ALL HERE FOR YOUR CONVENIENCE.

1. 2. 3. 4. 5. 6. 7. 8. 9. 10. 11. 12. 13. 14. 15. 16. 17. 18. 19. 20. 21. 22. 23. 24. 25. 26. 27. 28. 29. 30. 31. 32. 33. 34. 35. 36. 37. 38. 39. 40. 41. 42. 43. 44. 45. 46. 47. 48. 49. 50. 51. 52. 53. 54. 55. 56. 57. 58. 59. 60. 61. 62. 63. 64. 65. 66. 67. 68. 69. 70. 71. 72. 73. 74. 75. 76. 77. 78. 79. 80. 81. 82. 83. 84. 85. 86. 87. 88. 89. 90. 91. 92. 93. 94. 95. 96. 97. 98. 99. 100. 101. 102. 103. 104. 105. 106. 107. 108. 109. 110. 111. 112. 113. 114. 115. 116. 117. 118. 119. 120. 121. 122. 123. 124. 125. 126. 127. 128. 129. 130. 131. 132. 133. 134. 135. 136. 137. 138. 139. 140. 141. 142. 143. 144. 145. 146. 147. 148. 149. 150. 151. 152. 153. 154. 155. 156. 157. 158. 159. 160. 161. 162. 163. 164. 165. 166. 167. 168. 169. 170. 171. 172. 173. 174. 175. 176. 177. 178. 179. 180. 181. 182. 183. 184. 185. 186. 187. 188. 189. 190. 191. 192. 193. 194. 195. 196. 197. 198. 199. 200. 201. 202. 203. 204. 205. 206. 207. 208. 209. 210. 211. 212. 213. 214. 215. 216. 217. 218. 219. 220. 221. 222. 223. 224. 225. 226. 227. 228. 229. 230. 231. 232. 233. 234. 235. 236. 237. 238. 239. 240. 241. 242. 243. 244. 245. 246. 247. 248. 249. 250. 251. 252. 253. 254. 255. 256. 257. 258. 259. 260. 261. 262. 263. 264. 265. 266. 267. 268. 269. 270. 271. 272. 273. 274. 275. 276. 277. 278. 279. 280. 281. 282. 283. 284. 285. 286. 287. 288. 289. 290. 291. 292. 293. 294. 295. 296. 297. 298. 299. 300. 301. 302. 303. 304. 305. 306. 307. 308. 309. 310. 311. 312. 313. 314. 315. 316. 317. 318. 319.

AND NOW, WITHOUT FURTHER ADO, PLEASE ALLOW ME TO INTRODUCE THE...

...INTRODUCTION:

YOU'RE A DICK AND SO AM I.

I ONCE HEARD THAT PEOPLE OFTEN COME TO BLOWS BECAUSE
THEY CAN'T BELIEVE EACH OTHER'S LEVEL OF STUPIDITY.
THAT'S RIGHT, EVEN THOUGH WE'RE LIVING IN THE DIGITAL
INFORMATION AGE OF SMART TECH AND ADVANCED COMMUNICATION,
MANY HUMANS STILL THINK A VIABLE SOLUTION AT TIMES
IS TO SMASH THEIR FIST INTO ANOTHER PERSON'S NOSE.
THAT'S BECAUSE NO MATTER HOW HARD WE TRY, WE'RE ALWAYS GOING
TO ANNOY SOMEONE ABOUT SOMETHING. YOU MAY NOT AGREE AND FIND
THAT LAST STATEMENT ANNOYING. (IF SO, D'YOU SEE MY POINT?)
THE FACT IS, IF YOU THINK YOU'RE NEVER ANNOYING, THAT'S ACTUALLY
VERY ANNOYING. JUST ASK THE CLOSEST PERSON TO YOU. THEY'LL
EASILY BE ABLE TO LIST THE THINGS YOU DO THAT DRIVE THEM CRAZY,
BUT THEY LET THOSE GO, BELIEVING THAT YOUR REDEEMING
QUALITIES OUTWEIGH YOUR SKIDDED, SHAME-FILLED UNDERWEAR
LEFT STUCK TO THE BEDROOM FLOOR (AGAIN).
TESTING THE PATIENCE OF OTHERS COMES AS NATURAL TO US AS
BREATHING (ESPECIALLY HEAVY MOUTH-BREATHING, OR MAYBE A
NOSE WHISTLE). IT'S JUST SOMETHING WE DO TO EACH OTHER
AT HOME, AT WORK, DURING OUR COMMUTE, OR AT AN EVENT.
EVEN ON VACATION THERE'S NO ESCAPE FROM SOME IGNORANT
PRICK/PRICKESS BEING TOO LOUD BECAUSE THEY'RE SO EXCITED
TO BE ENJOYING A BREAK FROM THE PEOPLE WHO ANNOY <u>THEM</u>.
THIS CONSTANT ANNOYANCE IS THE FUEL THAT POWERS THE DAILY
BLOG CONTENT THAT WEEPS FROM THE IRRITATED SORES IN MY MIND.
IT'S THE TRAIT OF HUMANITY THAT BREEDS MY PROFANITY.
SO, IF ANYTHING IN THIS BOOK ANNOYS YOU, THEN GOOD. IT SERVES YOU
RIGHT FOR BEING SUCH AN ANNOYING DICK IN THE FIRST PLACE.

LET THE RANDOMNESS BEGIN...

THE ONLY WAY 99.9% OF US COULD BECOME "LEGENDARY" IS IF WE DO SOMETHING MOMENTOUSLY STUPID.

I LIKE MANY PEOPLE, EXCEPT MOST OF THEM.

IF YOU CAN'T BEAT THEM, JOIN THEM.

THEN DESTROY THEM FROM THE INSIDE.

PARRONTS

—A parrot's parents.

NEED A BIG IDEA.

ORGANIZE A COMMITTEE.

CREATE A MEETING OF MINDS.

HEAR EVERYONE'S PERSPECTIVE.

LEARN EVERYONE HAS A DIFFERENT OPINION.

REALIZE NO ONE AGREES ON ANYTHING.

FIND MORE PROBLEMS THAN SOLUTIONS.

STRAIN EVEN MORE RELATIONSHIPS.

THANK EVERYONE FOR THEIR TIME.

SWEAR TO NEVER ORGANIZE A COMMITTEE AGAIN.

RETURN TO DESK.

SOLVE IT YOUR FUCKING SELF.

FLYING WOULD BE MORE FUN
IF EVERY PASSENGER HAD AN EJECTOR SEAT

MINI STORAGE

—A bad name for a brothel.

WHEN YOU DON'T FEEL LIKE PUTTING IN THE EFFORT, REMEMBER THERE'S A SPECIES OF OCTOPUS THAT DETACHES ITS PENIS AND JUST THROWS IT IN THE FEMALE'S DIRECTION.

STAY MOTIVATED.

DON'T BE A DICKLESS OCTOPUS.

I EXERCISE FOR THE BODY I HAVE,

NOT THE BODY
I WANT.

DO YOU ALWAYS EXPECT MORE THAN TWO CHOICES?

1. YES
2. NO
3. YES

GOD: "I SHALL GIVE YOU A PROTECTIVE SHELL."

CRAB: "SOUNDS GOOD!"

GOD: "I SHALL GIVE YOU TWO STRONG CLAWS."

CRAB: "ALRIGHT!"

GOD: "I SHALL GIVE YOU SIX ARMORED LEGS."

CRAB: "NICE!"

GOD: "YOU SHALL WALK IN A SIDEWAYS DIRECTION."

CRAB: "WHAT? YOU'RE KIDDING, RIGHT?"

GOD: "NO. YOU SHALL WALK SIDEWAYS."

CRAB: "WHAT THE FUCK?"

GOD: "THERE'S NO NEED TO BE SO...CRABBY."

CRAB: "I'M GOING TO LOOK LIKE A TOTAL PRICK WALKING SIDEWAYS."

GOD: "YOU SHALL BE UNIQUE."

CRAB: "UNIQUE? WHY DON'T YOU GIVE ME EYES ON STALKS WHILE YOU'RE AT IT!"

GOD: "I LIKE YOUR THINKING."

CRAB: "OH, FOR FUCK'S SAKE."

GOD: "I DON'T LIKE YOUR TONE, SO I SHALL REMOVE YOUR VOICE."

CRAB:

HOW I EXPLAINED PUBERTY TO MY KIDS

"IMAGINE ALL OF YOUR HORMONES ARE SNOWFLAKES IN A SNOW GLOBE.

PUBERTY GIVES IT A GOOD SHAKE, SO YOUR HORMONES FLY ALL OVER THE PLACE.

THEN, WHEN THEY FINALLY SETTLE DOWN, THE SNOWMAN HAS A HAIRY DICK."

THERE'S A VAST DIFFERENCE BETWEEN LIVING <u>THE</u> BEST LIFE AND LIVING <u>YOUR</u> BEST LIFE.

IF I HAD THERAPY, I'D NEED A SECOND THERAPIST TO HELP ME MENTALLY COPE WITH THE BILLS FROM THE FIRST THERAPIST.

LABIARINTH

—When you can't find the clitoris.

MY 9-YEAR-OLD SON:

"I WOULD FLY A PLANE INTO A BAD PERSON'S HEAD, BUT I WOULDN'T BE FLYING IT. I'D TRAIN AN INDESTRUCTIBLE MONKEY TO FLY IT, AND WHEN THE POLICE SHOWED UP, I'D JUST SAY I'D NEVER SEEN THE INDESTRUCTIBLE MONKEY BEFORE."

ME:

"I DON'T THINK YOU WANT TO GET ON THE BAD SIDE OF AN INDESTRUCTIBLE MONKEY."

MY 9-YEAR-OLD SON:

"HMM...DID YOU KNOW I'VE GOT MY OWN PRIVATE TOOTHPASTE."

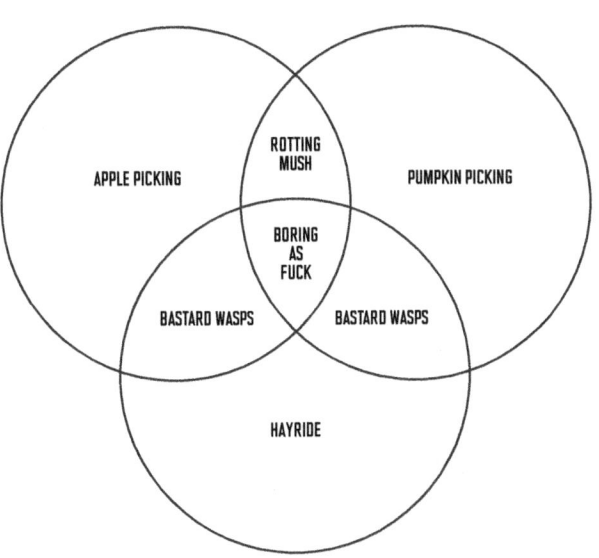

WELCOME TO NURSERY RHYME TIME

HERE WE GO ROUND THE MULBERRY BUSH,
THE MULBERRY BUSH,
THE MULBERRY BUSH.
HERE WE GO ROUND THE MULBERRY BUSH,
WE WISH SUSAN MULBERRY
WOULD WAX THAT SHIT.

LITTLE JACK HORNER
SAT IN THE CORNER,
EATING A CHRISTMAS PIE.
HE PUT IN HIS THUMBS,
RUBBED THE JUICE ON HIS PLUMS,
AND SAID, "WHAT A KINKY BOY AM I!"

FIVE LITTLE MONKEYS JUMPING ON THE BED,
ONE FELL OFF AND BUMPED HIS HEAD.
MAMA CALLED THE DOCTOR
AND THE DOCTOR SAID,
"MRS. WILSON, IF YOU CONTINUE TO HAVE SEX
WITH ANIMALS, I'LL HAVE TO REPORT YOU."

LITTLE MISS MUFFET,
SAT ON A TUFFET,
EATING HER CURDS AND WHEY.
ALONG CAME A SPIDER,
WHO SAT DOWN BESIDE HER,
AND SAID,
"WHAT THE FUCK IS THAT
NASTY SHIT YOU'RE EATING?"

JACK AND JILL WENT UP THE HILL
TO FETCH A PAIL OF WATER.
JACK FELL DOWN AND BROKE HIS CROWN,
SO JILL STARTED DATING A GUY NAMED PAUL
WHO SHE MET IN THE PUB.

OH THE GRAND OLD DUKE OF YORK,
HE HAD TEN THOUSAND MEN,
HE MARCHED THEM UP TO THE TOP OF THE HILL
AND HE MARCHED THEM DOWN AGAIN.
AND WHEN THEY WERE UP, THEY WERE UP,
AND WHEN THEY WERE DOWN, THEY WERE DOWN.
AND WHEN THEY WERE ONLY HALFWAY UP,
THEY WONDERED, "WHY ARE WE MARCHING
FOR THIS FUCKING CLOWN?"

TODAY, I SAW
A MAN ANGRILY
SHOUTING AT A PIGEON.

THERE'S A
STRONG CHANCE
IT WAS A CASE OF
MISTAKEN IDENTITY.

**EVERY DAY,
I'M THANKFUL FOR:**

**PRIVATE JETS,
EXCLUSIVE COUNTRY CLUBS,
YACHTS,
PENTHOUSES,
SECLUDED MANSIONS,
VIP AREAS, AND
LUXURY ISLAND VACATIONS,**

**BECAUSE THEY KEEP MANY
RICH, SPOILED,
RED-TROUSER-WEARING
PRICKS AWAY FROM ME.**

DECISION OF THE DAY

SEND A DICK PIC
OR
ERECT A CAREER?

THE MALE OSTRICH CAN ROAR LIKE A LION.

WOW, THOSE GUYS MUST REALLY FUCK WITH EACH OTHER.

THE INCREDIBLE HULK'S TESTICLES
3 FOR $5

PRINT THIS OUT AND PLACE IT WITH THE AVOCADOS IN A GROCERY STORE.

"SUSAN HOSTS GREAT DINNER PARTIES, BUT IT CAN'T BE EASY WITH HER SHORT ARMS."

—How the Lazy Susan was invented.

YOUNGER

"ONE DAY, ALL OF THIS WILL BE MINE."

OLDER

"NONE OF THAT WILL EVER BE MINE. NOW WHERE DID I PUT THAT LAST CAN OF BEANS?"

IF YOU CAN SAY,
"FUCK YOU"
IN A POLITE WAY,
YOU HAVE A
GREAT FUTURE IN
CUSTOMER SERVICE.

HOW TO KEEP YOUR MARRIAGE FRESH AND ALIVE:

KEEP GETTING MARRIED.

TURDLES

—Obstacles in your way when you're rushing to the bathroom.

I OFTEN END AN EMAIL WITH
"HAPPY TO DISCUSS"
BECAUSE ENDING IT WITH
"JUST LEAVE IT AND MOVE ON
YOU INTERFERING PRICK"
MAY NOT BE WELL RECEIVED.

I'M STARTING A CULT OF ONE.

WHO'S WITH ME?

NOBODY?

PERFECT.

WHENEVER I'M ACCUSED OF HAVING A TROPHY WIFE, I'M RELIEVED SHE CAN'T HEAR THROUGH THE GLASS OF THE DISPLAY CASE.

WHEN I HEARD ABOUT

WHO COULD SHOOT

FROM HER VAGINA

WONDERED IF I COULD

A WOMAN IN BANGKOK

PING-PONG BALLS

MY COMPETITIVE SIDE

RETURN HER SERVE

IF A MEDICAL PROFESSIONAL USES THE WORD "STIFFY," THAT'S NOT A MEDICAL PROFESSIONAL.

SOMETIMES, I FEEL LIKE I'VE GOT MY SHIT TOGETHER AND NOPE, IT'S GONE.

I HAVE
STONED THOUGHTS
ON JUST OXYGEN.

MAYBE I SHOULD
STOP INHALING.

SOME PEOPLE
PRONOUNCE IT AS "GIF".

OTHER PEOPLE
PRONOUNCE IT AS "GIF".

BUT I THINK
IT SHOULD BE "GIF".

TO FULLY EMBRACE LIFE,
WE MUST
LIVE IN THE MOMENT.

WE MUST PUT DOWN OUR PHONES RIGHT NOW AND OH LOOK! A FUN QUIZ THAT WILL TELL ME WHICH TYPE OF SAUSAGE MATCHES MY PERSONALITY!

COCK BLOCK

REMEMBER THAT TIME AT COLLEGE WHEN YOUR ANNOYING HOUSEMATE HADN'T GOT LAID FOR THREE YEARS, AND WHEN HE FINALLY BROUGHT A GIRL HOME, YOU'D COVERED HIS BEDROOM WALLS IN PAGES FROM AN OLD PORNO MAGAZINE THAT FEATURED WOMEN WITH FERAL PUBIC REGIONS THAT EACH RESEMBLED A YETI'S BUTTCRACK, SO THE GIRL IMMEDIATELY LEFT THE HOUSE WITHOUT SAYING A SINGLE WORD AND YOUR HOUSEMATE TOTALLY LOST HIS SHIT? NO? JUST ME THEN

IF YOU GET NAKED
AND JUMP UP AND DOWN
IN FRONT OF A MIRROR,
YOU CAN SEE EXACTLY
WHAT YOU NEED TO LOSE...

THE MIRROR.

"AND AS YOU CAN SEE, THE HANDS ARE IN A PERMANENT JERK-OFF POSITION."

—Chief LEGO designer presenting the first ever Minifigure.

STICK INSECT:	"IS THAT IT? AM I COMPLETE?"
GOD:	"YES, YOU'RE PERFECT."
STICK INSECT:	"WHAT DO I DO EXACTLY?"
GOD:	"YOU WALK ABOUT SLOWLY, AND IF YOU SEE ANY PREDATORS, YOU STAY STILL."
STICK INSECT:	"SO THEY THINK I'M A STICK?"
GOD:	"YES."
STICK INSECT:	"WHAT ELSE DO I DO?"
GOD:	"WELL, THAT'S KIND OF IT REALLY."
STICK INSECT:	"I JUST LOOK LIKE A STICK AND ACT LIKE A STICK?"
GOD:	"YES."
STICK INSECT:	"SO, I'M BASICALLY A STICK THAT LIVES IN CONSTANT FEAR OF BEING EATEN?"
GOD:	"YES, BUT IF YOU DO FIND A FEMALE, YOU'LL HAVE SEX FOR WEEKS."
STICK INSECT:	"REALLY? THAT'S AWESOME!"
GOD:	"YOU'RE WELCOME."
STICK INSECT:	"AND WHAT DOES ONE OF THESE SEXY LADIES LOOK LIKE?"
GOD:	"A STICK."
STICK INSECT:	"WHAT? SO WHAT ARE MY CHANCES OF FINDING ONE?"
GOD:	"SLIM TO NONE, AND SLIM'S OUT OF TOWN."
STICK INSECT:	"YOU CAN BE SUCH A DICK SOMETIMES."
GOD:	"BETTER THAN BEING A STICK."
STICK INSECT:	"WHAT?! YOU MOTHERFUC..."
GOD:	"ENOUGH! NOW GO, BEFORE I GIVE YOU BIG RED BALLS THAT LOOK LIKE JUICY BERRIES."

"NO FUCKS GIVEN."

—A eunuch with attitude.

THERE ARE 3 TYPES OF PEOPLE IN THE WORLD:

1. THOSE WHO RUN MARATHONS.
2. THOSE WHO DON'T EVEN HAVE THE ENERGY TO THINK OF A 3RD TYPE OF PERSON.
3. SEE ABOVE.

QUESTIONS TO ASK AT PARTIES WHEN YOU'RE BORED

HAVE YOU EVER SEEN A CAT'S ASSHOLE OPEN
WHEN IT FARTS?

IF YOU HAD TO HAVE A CAGE FIGHT ON TV,
WOULD YOU FEEL SELF-CONSCIOUS
ABOUT YOUR NIPPLES?

IF YOU SAW A KID FALL INTO A TIGER ENCLOSURE,
HOW LONG WOULD YOU FILM IT BEFORE GETTING HELP?

WOULD YOU DONATE YOUR LEFT ARM FOR $100 MILLION
IF YOU HAD TO TELL EVERYONE YOU WON THE MONEY
IN VEGAS ON A ONE-ARMED BANDIT?

DO YOU THINK FINGER PUPPETS
ARE A GATEWAY TO BESTIALITY?

IF YOU HAD A JETPACK, WOULD YOU FEEL
LIKE A TOTAL PRICK ON YOUR COMMUTE?

IF A FRIEND REVEALED HE HAD TWO PENISES,
HOW WOULD YOU NOT LAUGH WHEN HE SHOWED YOU?

IF A PASSING SQUIRREL CALLED YOU "A CRAZY CUNT,"
WOULD YOU TELL ANYONE?

MR. VENN MOONING

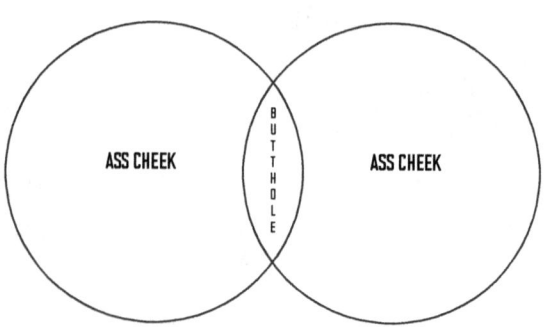

PEOPLE

THOSE WHO GET OUT OF THE POOL TO PEE.

PEEPLE

THOSE WHO GET INTO THE POOL TO PEE.

MY MOTHER IS GOING THROUGH THE CHANGE.

SO FAR, SHE HAS $3.75 TOWARDS A LIP WAX.

THAT FEELING INSIDE

THERE'S NO TIME FOR REFLECTION
WHEN A MAN WHO HATES REJECTION
SPOTS YOUR MORNING ERECTION
IN A FACILITY OF CORRECTION

THERE'S NO TIME FOR REFLECTION
AS HE TRIES TO MAKE A CONNECTION
TO YOUR INVOLUNTARY PROJECTION
THAT REFUSES TO EVADE DETECTION

THERE'S NO TIME FOR REFLECTION
BECAUSE YOU CHEATED IN THAT ELECTION
THEN FOLLOWED YOUR WIFE'S DIRECTION
TO NOT PAY "BIG BARRY" FOR PROTECTION

WEEKLY WORKOUT

- **MON:** PUSH-UPS / CRUNCHES
- **TUES:** PUSH-UPS / CRUNCHES / SQUATS
- **WED:** PUSH-UPS / CRUNCHES / SQUATS / JERK OFF
- **THUR:** PUSH-UPS / CRUNCHES / JERK OFF / JERK OFF
- **FRI:** PUSH-UPS / JERK OFF / JERK OFF / JERK OFF
- **SAT:** JERK OFF / JERK OFF / JERK OFF / JERK OFF
- **SUN:** REST (JUST KIDDING) / JERK OFF

IF PUBLIC SPEAKING MAKES YOU NERVOUS, JUST IMAGINE THE AUDIENCE IMAGINING YOU NAKED.

**C'MON GARRY,
DO YOU REALLY NEED
THAT SECOND "R"?**

ME:
"GOOD LUCK WITH YOUR SCIENCE TEST TODAY."

MY DAUGHTER:
"I'LL TRY."

ME:
"NO, YOU'LL SUCCEED."

MY DAUGHTER:
"YOU CAN'T SUCCEED WITHOUT TRYING."

ME:
"DEPENDS HOW RICH YOUR PARENTS ARE."

JUST WHEN I THOUGHT
I WAS MORALLY BANKRUPT,
I FOUND $120 IN MY
GRANDMA'S HANDBAG.

AFTER THE SUCCESS OF FINGERLESS GLOVES, IT'S TIME TO LAUNCH MY TOELESS SOCKS.

I WOULD NEVER HAVE A THREESOME.

I PREFER TO DISAPPOINT MY LOVERS ONE AT A TIME.

POOFINGER

—The Bond villain nobody mentions.

I HAVE TWO SPEEDS:

50% MINIMUM EFFORT
AND
50% MAXIMUM EFFORT

**"BRING YOUR CHILD TO WORK DAY"
IS ALWAYS FOLLOWED BY
"WHAT THE FUCK WERE WE THINKING DAY."**

OVER-THE-HILLENNIALS

—People who refer to themselves as Millennials, but they're old as fuck.

S'MORONS

—Parents who get excited
about making s'mores.

THERE WAS ONCE
A SPECIES OF CROCODILE
THAT COULD GALLOP.

BEING A JOCKEY MUST
HAVE BEEN A SHITTY JOB.

SMELL IS ONE OF THE BIGGEST TRIGGERS OF MEMORY.

HOW WILL YOU BE REMEMBERED?

DURING YOUR LIFETIME, YOU WILL PRODUCE ENOUGH SALIVA TO FILL TWO SWIMMING POOLS.
AND GET BANNED FROM TWO COUNTRY CLUBS.

WRITE DRUNK, EDIT DRUNKER.

THANKS TO THE MISINFORMATION HIGHWAY, YOU CAN NOW CHOOSE YOUR OWN FACTS. WE'RE ALL AS MISINFORMED AS EACH OTHER, BUT WITH OPPOSING VIEWS. IN FACT, WE'VE NEVER HAD SO MUCH BULLSHIT INSTANTLY AVAILABLE AT OUR FINGERTIPS. THERE IS NO TRUSTED SOURCE ANYWHERE. MOST PEOPLE DON'T READ PAST THE HEADLINE, WHICH IS OFTEN A BLESSING IN DISGUISE. THE TRUTH HURTS, BUT A LACK OF TRUTH HURTS MORE. YOU'RE ONLY FED EXACTLY WHAT YOU WANT TO HEAR BECAUSE YOUR BROWSING HABITS FABRICATED YOUR ALGORITHM, AND NOW IT'S CONTINUALLY SHAPING YOU TO BELIEVE MORE OF THE SAME. THE MORE YOUR OPINION IS CONFIRMED, THE MORE ONE-SIDED YOU BECOME. THE OTHER SIDE ARE DELUDED AND WRONG. THEY ARE THE WEAK-MINDED FOOLS BEING MANIPULATED BY THE MEDIA, NOT YOU. YOU'RE THE INFORMED ONE WITH ALL OF THE FACTS. AND HOW DO YOU KNOW YOU'RE RIGHT? YOU READ IT ON THE INTERNET.

MY WIFE:	"THAT ANT IS UP LATE."
ME:	"WHAT D'YOU MEAN?"
MY WIFE:	"I SAW HIM THIS MORNING."
ME:	"WAIT...YOU THINK THAT'S THE SAME ANT YOU SAW 14 HOURS AGO?"
MY WIFE:	"IT COULD BE."
ME:	"HOW D'YOU KNOW THEY DON'T WORK SHIFTS?
MY WIFE:	"HMM...MAYBE. ANTS ARE SO TOUGH. I JUST KICKED THAT ANT OFF THE DECK AND NOW HE'S BACK."
ME:	"AGAIN, HOW D'YOU KNOW THAT'S THE SAME ANT?"
MY WIFE:	"I DON'T, BUT IT PROBABLY IS."

I THINK ABOUT DISCUSSING PROBABILITY, BUT DECIDE TO SAY NOTHING AND RETURN TO READING MY BOOK.

"I THINK WE SHOULD SNIFF OTHER BUTTHOLES."

—A dog trying to end a long-term relationship.

FLAT EARTHERS EXIST ALL AROUND THE WORLD.

"NOTHING TASTES AS GOOD AS SKINNY FEELS."

—Supermodel

"NOTHING FEELS AS GOOD AS SKINNY TASTES."

—Supercannibal

POISON DART FROG:	"WOW! LOOK AT MY AMAZING COLOR!"
GOD:	"YES, YOU ARE A MAGNIFICENT BLUE."
POISON DART FROG:	"WILL I LIVE AMONG BRIGHT BLUE PLANTS, SO I'M NICE AND HIDDEN?"
GOD:	"NO, THE PLANTS ARE GREEN."
POISON DART FROG:	"WHAT? BUT I'LL STAND OUT LIKE A BRIGHT BLUE DUMBASS."
GOD:	"YES, BUT I'VE MADE YOU EXTREMELY POISONOUS, SO PREDATORS WILL LEAVE YOU ALONE."
POISON DART FROG:	"HOW WILL THEY KNOW I'M POISONOUS?"
GOD:	"WELL, WHEN THEY'VE EATEN YOU, THEY'LL DIE."
POISON DART FROG:	(AWKWARD SILENCE)
GOD:	"OTHER ANIMALS WILL SEE THEM DIE AND LEARN NOT TO EAT BRIGHTLY COLORED FROGS.
POISON DART FROG:	(AWKWARD SILENCE)
GOD:	"ARE YOU OK?"
POISON DART FROG:	"NO, I'M NOT FUCKING OK."
GOD:	"WHY NOT?"
POISON DART FROG:	"BECAUSE I HAVE TO GET EATEN FOR OTHER PREDATOR PRICKS TO LEARN."
GOD:	"AH, I SEE."
POISON DART FROG:	"WHAT IF YOU MADE 2,000 MORE LIKE ME AND SENT THEM OUT FIRST?"
GOD:	"I COULD, BUT WHAT IF THEY ASK ME THE SAME QUESTION?"
POISON DART FROG:	"TELL THEM TO HIDE IN THE BRIGHT BLUE PLANTS."
GOD:	"I WON'T LIE, BUT I WILL SEND OUT 2,000 BRIGHTLY COLORED FROGS BEFORE YOU."
POISON DART FROG:	"GREAT! THANKS DUDE."

(GOD SENDS OUT 1,000 BRIGHT RED FROGS AND 1,000 BRIGHT YELLOW FROGS.)

SAY IT LIKE YOU MEME IT.

I DONNY KNOW WHY AUTOCORRECT CHANGES THE WORD DONNY TO DONNY.

I DONNY KNOW ANYONE NAMED DONNY AND I HAVE NEVER INTENTIONALLY TYPED DONNY ANYWHERE AT ANYTIME.

I DONNY THINK IT'S A HUGE DEAL, BUT IT DOES MAKE IT HARD TO WRITE A LIST OF DOS AND DONNYS.

A POULTRY LITTLE POEM

DON'T STICK YOUR DICK IN,
AN UNCOOKED CHICKEN,
FOR THE SAKE OF RHYME.

DON'T SCREW THE MENU,
WHEN ALL CHEFS TELL YOU,
TRUE LOVE COMES WITH THYME.

VAGNINJA

—A vagina that
sneaks up on you when
you least expect it.

SEXY PEOPLE HAVE
"COME TO BED" EYES.

I HAVE
"NEED TO GO TO BED" EYES.

MANY GUYS
ADMIT TO BEING
A BREAST MAN,
AN ASS MAN,
OR A LEG MAN.

BUT SOME FREAKS
DON'T EVEN
FIND CHICKENS
SEXUALLY AROUSING.

IF I'D BEEN A MEDIEVAL TORTURER OPERATING THE RACK, I'D WEAR A T-SHIRT WITH THE SLOGAN, "WHAT DOESN'T KILL YOU ONLY MAKES YOU LONGER."

THERE ARE 2 DEFAULT
APPS IN OUR HEADS:

THE "YOU'RE GREAT" APP
AND
THE "YOU'RE SHIT" APP.

BUT IF YOU DOWNLOAD
THE FREE
"FUCK OFF DOUBT" APP
TO DELETE THE
"YOU'RE SHIT" APP,
YOUR O.S. WILL RUN SMOOTHER.

HOW THE GRAPEFRUIT GOT ITS NAME

"IS IT THE SAME SIZE AS A GRAPE?"
"NO."

"DOES IT TASTE LIKE A GRAPE?"
"NO."

"CAN YOU EAT ITS SKIN LIKE A GRAPE?"
"NO."

"DOES IT GROW ON A VINE LIKE A GRAPE?"
"NO."

"IS IT CLASSED AS A FRUIT?"
"YES."

"THEN WE SHALL CALL IT, THE GRAPEFRUIT."

"HEY, SHUT THE FUCK UP! IT'S ONLY 6AM!"

"FUCK YOU, SEED BRAIN! AND KEEP YOUR DAMN NOISE DOWN!"

"WILL YOU TWO FEATHERED FUCKHEADS SHUT YOUR DUMBASS BEAK HOLES!"

"HEY, SELFISH SHITBAGS, STOP YOUR FUCKING SHOUTING!"

"WILL YOU NOISY WINGED FUCKWITS STICK A FUCKING WORM IN IT!"

"EVERY DAMN DAY, YOU TREE-LOVING TWATS JUST WAKE UP SPOUTING SHIT!"

"SERIOUSLY? YOU PERCHING PRICKS STARTED THIS MORNING BULLSHIT AGAIN?!"

—What birds are actually saying when you hear them "singing" in the morning.

I JUST GOT FIRED FROM A NUDIST RESORT.

MY BOSS AND I NEVER SAW EYE-TO-EYE.

SOME PEOPLE EAT THEIR FEELINGS. MINE TASTE TOO BITTER.

MY MOTHER-IN-LAW:
"I GET WRINKLES ON MY FACE FROM ALWAYS SLEEPING ON THE SAME SIDE."

MY WIFE:
"HUH...WHICH SIDE?"

ME:
"THE FRONT SIDE."

GROWING UP, I HAD AN IMAGINARY FRIEND.

TODAY, I HAVE HUNDREDS OF THEM.

THANKS FACEBOOK.

IF YOU NEED ANYTHING (AND I DO MEAN ANYTHING), JUST ASK AND I'LL BE HAPPY TO IGNORE YOU.

QUESTIONS I'VE ASKED A PEST EXTERMINATOR

SOMEONE HAS BEEN USING MY EXPENSIVE SHAMPOO...
CAN YOU CHECK MY SHOWER FOR REALLY HAIRY BUGS?

IF I INVENTED TINY, INDIVIDUAL ANT TRAPS,
LIKE MOUSETRAPS, HOW MANY WOULD YOU NEED?

IF YOU COULD FLY, WOULD IT MAKE YOUR JOB EASIER?

DO GRASSHOPPERS PERFORM AN OFFICIAL HANDOVER
TO CRICKETS FOR THE NIGHTTIME SHIFT?

IF I LEFT OUT CLEAR INSTRUCTIONS,
WOULD CARPENTER ANTS FIX MY FENCE?

ARE YOU IMMUNE TO BUG SPRAY?

WOULD YOU MIND QUIETLY SITTING NEXT TO ME
ON 'WASP WATCH' WHILE I FINISH THIS BOOK?

HAVE YOU EVER BEEN FOOLED INTO TAKING BAIT HOME
AND INADVERTENTLY KILLED YOUR WHOLE FAMILY?

I'M KIND
OF A DICK.

IF YOU'RE STRUGGLING TO LOSE WEIGHT:

1. BUY A MASSIVE PAIR OF JEANS.

2. WEAR THEM FOR 10 MINUTES.

3. TAKE THEM OFF.

4. SMILE FOR A PHOTO HOLDING THE JEANS IN FRONT OF YOUR LEGS.

5. ADD THE CAPTION: "WON'T BE NEEDING THESE ANYMORE!"

6. CELEBRATE BY EATING AN ENTIRE CHOCOLATE CAKE.

RACISM IS LEARNED BEHAVIOR TAUGHT BY IGNORANT PEOPLE.

LET'S MAKE SURE THE IGNORANT ARE EDUCATED BY THE EDUCATED.

FAILING THAT, LET THE IGNORANT TEACH THE IGNORANT HOW TO SKYDIVE.

A BETTER NAME
FOR A UROLOGIST
IS A DICKTOR.

ALWAYS READ THE SMALL PRINT.*

*YOU SUBSERVIENT PISSFLAP.

AFTER SEX, I LIKE TO LIE BACK AND BASK IN THE GLOW OF MY LOVER'S REGRET.

THE JOY OF
READING A BOOK
OF SHORT STORIES
IS IF YOU'RE
NOT ENJOYING ONE,
YOU'LL SOON BE
NOT ENJOYING
THE NEXT ONE.

A MOMENT OF HOPE

A WEALTHY OLD MAN SEATED HIMSELF IN A RESTAURANT FOR LUNCH.
A YOUNG WAITER APPROACHED TO TAKE HIS ORDER.
IN THE HOPE IT WOULD EARN HIM A BIG TIP,
THE WAITER SPENT A LOT OF EFFORT
RECOMMENDING THE BEST FOOD AND DRINK OPTIONS.
IN THE END, THE OLD MAN ORDERED JUST A SANDWICH AND A LEMONADE.
KNOWING THAT A SMALL BILL MEANT A SMALL TIP,
THE WAITER WALKED AWAY FEELING DISAPPOINTED.
AFTER FINISHING HIS MEAL, THE WEALTHY MAN
ASKED FOR THE CHECK.
WHEN THE WAITER PLACED THE BILL ON THE TABLE,
THE OLD MAN NOTICED THE SADNESS ON HIS FACE.
HE ASKED, "IS EVERYTHING OK, SON? ARE YOU HAVING A HARD DAY?"
THE WAITER REPLIED, "I'M HAVING A HARD LIFE, SIR."
AND WALKED AWAY.
WHEN HE RETURNED TO THE OLD MAN'S TABLE,
HE FOUND A TIP OF $10,000.

THE OLD MAN HAD JUST LEFT THE RESTAURANT,
SO THE WAITER RAN OUT TO CATCH HIM.
AS THE OLD MAN WAS GETTING INTO HIS CAR,
THE WAITER ASKED, "WHY DID YOU DO THIS?"
THE OLD MAN REPLIED, "WHEN I WAS YOUR AGE, I ALSO
STRUGGLED TO MAKE A LIVING AS A WAITER, BUT ONE DAY,
A WEALTHY MAN GAVE ME A SIMILAR TIP WHICH THEN
PAID FOR MY COLLEGE TUITION. I HOPE THIS MONEY
WILL HELP YOU AS IT ONCE HELPED ME."
THE YOUNG MAN WAS SPEECHLESS, AND THEN SAID,
"THESE DAYS, $10,000 DOESN'T EVEN COVER ONE YEAR
OF TUITION FEES. IT'S AT LEAST $30K."
THE SHOCKED OLD MAN REPLIED,
"YOU UNGRATEFUL LITTLE SHIT. I'M GONNA CALL YOUR
RESTAURANT AND TELL THEM IT WAS JUST A TYPO,
SO GOOD LUCK WITH YOUR $10, PUNK!"
THE WAITER SAID,
"FUCK YOU, YOU TIGHT OLD BASTARD!"
THE WEALTHY OLD MAN DROVE AWAY SHOUTING,
"GO FUCK YOURSELF, SANDWICH BITCH!"

IF THERE'S ALWAYS A
FIRST DANCE AT A WEDDING,
WHY ISN'T THERE A
LAST DANCE AT A FUNERAL?

NANO

—A very small grandmother.

**WHEN YOU SIT
OUTSIDE IN
THE SUMMER,
YOU BECOME
AN AIRPORT FOR**

BUGS.

SWEATY COLLEAGUE:
"UGH, I FEEL GROSS."

ME:
"IF IT'S ANY CONSOLATION,
YOU LOOK GROSS, TOO."

HR:
"SO, WE MEET AGAIN."

TOMORROW IS A BRAND NEW DAY, FULL OF MORE OPPORTUNITIES TO OVERPROMISE AND UNDER-DELIVER.

I'M PITCHING A NEW
TV SHOW CALLED,
"WHEN ANIMALS DON'T ATTACK."

IT MIGHT BE BORING,
BUT THE FOOTAGE IS REALLY
EASY TO CAPTURE.

MY WEAKNESSES ARE TOO STRONG FOR ME.

NO MATTER HOW
COLD IT GETS,
THERE'S ALWAYS ONE
ATTENTION-SEEKING
FUCKWIT
WEARING SHORTS.

THE ILLITERATI

—Privileged, dumbass, fuckheads whose rich parents paid for their grades, not their education.

Now they're "working" on their third failing start-up, like "McBeluga's Drive-thru Caviar Shack," "Deep End Me" (a pool boy dating app), or "Pizstick" (it's pizza, but on a stick).

I SEE YOU DEADLY SPIDER, WALKING ON THE PATH.
STAMP. MISS.
I SEE YOU ANNOYED SPIDER, WALKING UP MY SHOE.
SWING. MISS.
I SEE YOU ANGRY SPIDER, WALKING UP MY LEG.
SQUISH. MISS.
I SEE YOU FURIOUS SPIDER, WALKING UP MY BELLY.
SWAT. MISS.
I SEE YOU ENRAGED SPIDER, WALKING UP MY CHEST.
SPLAT. MISS.
I SEE YOU VENGEFUL SPIDER, WALKING UP MY FACE.
SLAP. MISS.
I SEE YOU VICTORIOUS SPIDER, WALKING ON THE PATH.
SLUR. YOU DIDN'T MISS.
I DON'T SEE YOU GLOATING SPIDER, WALKING ON MY GRAVE.

MOM:
"CAN YOU TUCK THEM IN TONIGHT?"

DAD:
"THE KIDS?"

MOM:
"NO, YOUR BALLS."

THIS SENTENCE IS FOR ALL THOSE WRITERS WHO FEAR THE BLANK PAGE.

QUARANTINE SECTION

CAUTION:
THE FOLLOWING PAGES WERE WRITTEN
DURING THE COVID-19 PANDEMIC.
BEFORE ENTERING THIS HAZARDOUS AREA,
PLEASE WEAR A MASK, WASH YOUR HANDS,
AND AVOID TOUCHING YOUR FACE.
TOUCHING YOUR GENITALS IS PERMITTED
AT YOUR OWN DISCRETION,
UNLESS YOU'RE MY UNCLE GREG.
(THAT GUY HAS GOT A SERIOUS PROBLEM.)

THE WORLD HAS LITERALLY GONE BATSHIT CRAZY

I RECENTLY DISCOVERED I'M MUCH MORE SOCIABLE FROM A DISTANCE

"KNOCK, KNOCK."
"FUCK OFF."

—A knock knock joke during lockdown.

IT'S HARD TO HAVE A WEEKEND WHEN THE WEEK DOESN'T END. IT'S HARD TO HAVE A WEEKEND WHEN THE WEEK DOESN'T END. IT'S HARD TO HAVE A WEEKEND WHEN THE WEEK DOESN'T END. IT'S HARD TO HAVE A WEEKEND WHEN THE WEEK DOESN'T END. IT'S HARD TO HAVE A WEEKEND WHEN THE WEEK DOESN'T END. IT'S HARD TO HAVE A WEEKEND WHEN THE WEEK DOESN'T END. IT'S HARD TO HAVE A WEEKEND WHEN THE WEEK DOESN'T END. IT'S HARD TO HAVE A WEEKEND WHEN THE WEEK DOESN'T END. IT'S HARD TO HAVE A WEEKEND WHEN THE WEEK DOESN'T END. IT'S HARD TO HAVE A WEEKEND WHEN THE WEEK DOESN'T END. IT'S HARD TO HAVE A WEEKEND WHEN THE WEEK DOESN'T END IT'S HARD TO HAVE A WEEKEND WHEN THE WEEK DOESN'T END. IT'S HARD TO HAVE A WEEKEND WHEN THE WEEK DOESN'T END. IT'S HARD TO HAVE A WEEKEND WHEN THE WEEK DOESN'T END. IT'S HARD TO HAVE A WEEKEND WHEN THE WEEK DOESN'T END. IT'S HARD TO HAVE A WEEKEND WHEN THE WEEK DOESN'T END. IT'S HARD TO HAVE A WEEKEND WHEN THE WEEK DOESN'T END. IT'S HARD TO HAVE A WEEKEND WHEN THE WEEK DOESN'T END. IT'S HARD TO HAVE A WEEKEND WHEN THE WEEK DOESN'T END. IT'S HARD TO HAVE A WEEKEND WHEN THE WEEK DOESN'T END. IT'S HARD TO HAVE A WEEKEND WHEN THE WEEK DOESN'T END. IT'S HARD TO HAVE A WEEKEND WHEN THE WEEK DOESN'T END IT'S HARD TO HAVE A WEEKEND WHEN THE WEEK DOESN'T END. IT'S HARD TO HAVE A WEEKEND WHEN THE WEEK DOESN'T END. IT'S HARD TO HAVE A WEEKEND WHEN THE WEEK DOESN'T END. IT'S HARD TO HAVE A WEEKEND WHEN THE WEEK DOESN'T END. IT'S HARD TO HAVE A WEEKEND WHEN THE WEEK DOESN'T END. IT'S HARD TO HAVE A WEEKEND WHEN THE WEEK DOESN'T END. IT'S HARD TO HAVE A WEEKEND WHEN THE WEEK DOESN'T END. IT'S HARD TO HAVE A WEEKEND WHEN THE WEEK DOESN'T END. IT'S HARD TO HAVE A WEEKEND WHEN THE WEEK DOESN'T END

SINCE THE LOCKDOWN STARTED, MY WIFE HAS BEEN GLUED TO HER DEVICE.

(I HATE THAT VIBRATOR.)

87% OF GYM MEMBERS DON'T EVEN KNOW THEIR GYM CLOSED.

"WHO THE FUCK TOOK MY CHARGER?"

—A game all the family can play.

AN ORGASM BOOSTS YOUR IMMUNE SYSTEM.

THAT'S WHY I'VE BEEN PANIC-MASTURBATING.

THE BATTERFLY EFFECT

THAT JUICY BAT LOOKS TASTY. ——————————— US STOCKS PLUMMET $5 TRILLION.

DURING LOCKDOWN, PLEASE SPARE A THOUGHT FOR ALL THOSE WHO DON'T HAVE FAMILY AT HOME, WHO DON'T HAVE A PARTNER TO CUDDLE-UP WITH, AND WHO DON'T HAVE KIDS TO PLAY WITH...

LUCKY BASTARDS.

WORKING FROM HOME DEMANDS BLOOD SWEATPANTS AND TEARS

SLOW THE FUCK DOWN

AS THE WORLD SPINS OUT OF CONTROL, STEP OFF FOR A MOMENT.
AND SLOW THE FUCK DOWN.
AS ANXIETY GRABS THE WHEEL, EXIT THE VEHICLE.
AND SLOW THE FUCK DOWN.
AS MANAGEMENT PANICS, ADD CALM TO THE BRAINSTORM.
AND SLOW THE FUCK DOWN.
AS YOU ZOOM FROM ONE VIDEO CALL TO ANOTHER, DISCONNECT.
AND SLOW THE FUCK DOWN.
AS YOUR HOME BECOMES YOUR PRISON, EMBRACE THE SANCTUARY.
AND SLOW THE FUCK DOWN.
AS THERE'S TOO MUCH TO PROCESS, SKIP TO THE END.
AND SLOW THE FUCK DOWN.
AS YOUR FINANCES FEEL SUFFOCATING, TAKE A DEEP BREATH.
AND SLOW THE FUCK DOWN.
AS THE MEDIA HYSTERIA SCREAMS FROM EVERY SCREEN, TURN IT OFF.
AND SLOW THE FUCK DOWN.
AS MISINFORMATION BECOMES YOUR ONLY SOURCE, TUNE IT OUT.
AND SLOW THE FUCK DOWN.
AS THE UNKNOWN THREATENS YOUR FUTURE, STAY SAFE FOR NOW.
AND. SLOW. THE. FUCK. DOWN.

THERE'S A REASON WHY I'M A "GLASS HALF FULL" KIND OF PERSON.

THAT'S ALL THAT WAS LEFT IN THE BOTTLE.

TO WHOM IT MAY CONCERN,

DUE TO BEING RESPONSIBLE FOR THE WELL-BEING AND EDUCATION OF MY CHILDREN,
I HAVE DECIDED TO TERMINATE MYSELF FROM HOMESCHOOLING FOR DRINKING ON THE JOB.
IT WAS COMPLETELY UNPROFESSIONAL,
TOTALLY UNDERSTANDABLE, AND I SINCERELY REGRET BEING ASSIGNED TO SUCH AN INCOMPATIBLE ROLE.
FINALLY, I WOULD LIKE TO WISH MY CHILDREN AND MY SPOUSE EVERY SUCCESS IN THEIR FUTURE ENDEAVORS.

SCIENTISTS CLAIM SHARKS ARE EVOLVING TO WALK ON LAND.

DON'T WORRY, WHEN THEY SEE THE STATE OF THE PLACE, THEY'LL FUCK OFF BACK TO THE OCEAN AS FAST AS THEIR LITTLE FIN-LEGS CAN CARRY THEM.

WHILE LOCKED DOWN, YOUR PARTNER DECIDES TO TAKE UP PAINTING AS A NEW HOBBY. YOUR PARTNER LOVES PAINTING, BUT THE ARTWORK THEY CREATE IS REALLY SHIT. AS THEY PROUDLY SHOW YOU THEIR PAINTINGS, YOU DON'T WANT TO HURT THEIR FEELINGS, SO YOU LIE AND TELL THEM HOW GREAT THEY ARE. INSPIRED BY YOUR PRAISE, THEY CREATE MORE PAINTINGS. EACH ONE IS AS SHIT AS THE LAST. AS YOU CONTINUE TO LIE AND FUEL THEIR CREATIVE OUTPUT, SOON THE PAINTINGS ARE FRAMED AND PLACED IN PRIME POSITIONS AROUND YOUR HOME. THEN THE LOCKDOWN ENDS, SO YOU INVITE FRIENDS OVER FOR A CELEBRATORY GET-TOGETHER. YOUR FRIENDS NOTICE ONE OF THE SHIT PAINTINGS AND POLITELY LIE ABOUT HOW GREAT IT IS. WHILE YOUR FRIENDS LIE TO YOU AND YOU LIE BACK TO THEM, YOUR PARTNER TRIES TO ACT ALL HUMBLE, BUT CAN'T RESIST TAKING YOUR FRIENDS ON A SHITTY TOUR TO SEE ALL THE SHIT PAINTINGS. YOU THEN HEAR YOUR FRIENDS POLITELY LIE TO YOUR PARTNER IN EVERY ROOM OF YOUR HOUSE. WHEN THE EVENING ENDS, YOU WATCH YOUR FRIENDS DRIVE AWAY KNOWING THAT'S THE LAST TIME YOU'LL EVER SEE THEM. YOU SLOWLY SHUT THE DOOR, TURN TO SEE YOUR PARTNER ENTHUSIASTICALLY OPENING A FRESH BOX OF NEW CANVASES, AND THINK, DURING THE LOCKDOWN, WHY THE FUCK DIDN'T I JUST PAY FOR NETFLIX?

10-YEAR-OLD SON:
"WHEN DO PEOPLE START PUBERTY?"

DAD:
"IT VARIES, BUT USUALLY AROUND 12 OR 13."

10-YEAR-OLD SON:
"IS THAT WHEN YOU GET A BIG BUSH?"

DAD:
"NO, THAT HAPPENS WHEN YOUR MOTHER'S IN LOCKDOWN."

AT OUR HOMESCHOOL, MY WIFE HAS ADOPTED THE ROLE OF "AMAZING TEACHER" AND I AM "THE ENTERTAINER," LIKE A SHITTY DRUNKEN CLOWN WHOSE BALLOON ANIMALS KEEP POPPING ON THE FIRST TWIST.

THESE DAYS, WE DON'T HEAR ABOUT ANYTHING OTHER THAN YOU-KNOW-WHAT, SO I WANTED TO WRITE A POST THAT DOESN'T EVEN MENTION IT. THE PROBLEM IS, EVEN THOUGH I HAVEN'T MENTIONED IT, YOU ALREADY KNOW WHAT I'M REFERENCING BECAUSE IT'S ALL YOU CAN THINK ABOUT RIGHT NOW, TOO. IN FACT, THIS IS SUCH A FUTILE EXERCISE, I MAY AS WELL JUST SAY IT: BUTT PLUG.

A PERSON WITH
A LAZY EYE
HAS A 50%
HIGHER CHANCE
OF LOOKING INTO
THE CAMERA
DURING A
ZOOM MEETING.

PROS AND CONS OF VIDEO CONFERENCING

PRO:
IT'S EASY TO HAVE MEETINGS WITH COLLEAGUES.

CON:
IT'S EASY TO HAVE MEETINGS WITH COLLEAGUES.

MY MICROWAVE IS A PRICK.

WHEN MY OATMEAL IS READY, IT BEEPS 4 TIMES.
4 FUCKING TIMES.
NOT 3.
NO, 3 WOULD HAVE BEEN PLENTY.
THAT 4TH BEEP IS OBNOXIOUS.
IT'S QUESTIONING MY INTELLIGENCE.
IT'S DOUBTING MY ABILITY TO HEAR 3 LOUD BEEPS.
IT'S FLIPPING ME THE MIDDLE FINGER THROUGH ITS
UNNECESSARY ELECTRONIC PRESENCE.
BUT THEN I REMEMBER ALL OF THE PEOPLE OUT THERE
SUFFERING FROM THE EFFECTS OF COVID-19,
POLICE BRUTALITY, AND SYSTEMIC RACISM,
WHICH MAKES ME HATE MYSELF FOR GETTING ANGRY
ABOUT A PATHETIC 4TH BEEP.
AND THEN I HATE THAT 4TH BEEP AGAIN FOR
MAKING ME HATE MYSELF.
I'VE SPENT TOO MUCH TIME AT HOME.

CHINBECILE

—An idiot who wears a face mask too low.

CORPORATE PEP TALK SOUNDBITES DURING THE PANDEMIC

"WE MUST DO EVERYTHING WE CAN TO KEEP DRIVING THE BUSINESS SIDEWAYS."

"NOW MORE THAN EVER, OUR NEXT MOVE MUST TAKE NOW TO NEXT TO BE THE NEXT NOW."

"WE MUST PREPARE FOR A 'NEW NORMAL' TO ENSURE WE ASPIRE TO 'NORMAL' AND REACH NEW HEIGHTS OF MEDIOCRITY."

"TO CUT UNNECESSARY SPENDING, WE'VE HIRED AN EXPENSIVE EFFICIENCY EXPERT TO RECOMMEND WHICH KEY EMPLOYEES SHOULD BE LAID OFF TO HELP PAY FOR THE EFFICIENCY REPORT."

"WE'RE ALL FUCKED, SO... UM... GO TEAM!"

☣

IF YOU DON'T BELIEVE IN SCIENCE, AT LEAST TRY TO MASK YOUR IGNORANCE.

"FOR FUCK'S SAKE CHEWIE, THE SHOWER'S ALL CLOGGED UP WITH HAIR AGAIN!"

"MWRRAGHSHUTTHEFUCKUPYOU WHINEYSHITWAISTCOATTWATWARRGH."

—Han (not so) Solo and Chewbacca in lockdown together.

ZOOM GUIDE FOR CALLING YOUR MOTHER

TIDY UP YOUR BACKGROUND.
CLEAN YOUR TEETH, FACE, AND CONSCIENCE.
BRUSH AT LEAST THE FRONT OF YOUR HAIR.
WEAR THE CLEANEST ITEM YOU OWN.
CALL HER.
REMIND HER HOW TO TURN HER CAMERA ON.
CONFIRM YOU CAN SEE HER 6 TIMES.
CONFIRM YOU CAN HEAR HER 6 TIMES.
TELL HER YOU MISS HER.
IGNORE HER SNARKY REPLY.
TAKE OCCASIONAL BITES OF SOMETHING HEALTHY.
APOLOGIZE FOR NOT SENDING A MOTHER'S DAY GIFT,
BUT YOU KNOW, CORONA.
IGNORE HER SNARKY REPLY.
TELL HER YOU GOTTA GO FOR...UM...AN ONLINE LANGUAGE CLASS?
YEAH, THAT SOUNDS GOOD.
TELL HER YOU'LL CALL HER AGAIN SOON.
CUT HER OFF TO AVOID ANOTHER SNARKY REPLY.
DON'T CALL HER AGAIN SOON.

IT'S OUR OWN FAULT, BUT NATURE FUCKING HATES US.

MY FRIEND ONCE SAW A NAKED OLD MAN DOING PUSH-UPS AND NOTICED THAT HIS BALLS NEVER LEFT THE FLOOR.

I'M SHARING THIS STORY JUST TO TAKE YOUR MIND OFF THIS BALLBAG OF A PANDEMIC FOR A MOMENT.

I'M GOING TO SELL 499-PIECE PUZZLES, AND IF ANY CUSTOMERS COMPLAIN ABOUT A MISSING PIECE, MY CUSTOMER RELATIONS TEAM WILL REPLY, "NO SHI."

THE DUMB AND THE DANGEROUS

—An action movie about the pandemic.

CORONAVIRUS OR NOT, CAN'T WE JUST NOMINATE PEOPLE TO BE QUARANTINED?

I COULD DO WITH A BREAK FROM BRANDON IN ACCOUNTS.

HEALTH OFFICIALS ARE CONCERNED ABOUT THE SPIKE IN CASES OF IDIOCY.

(WEAR A FUCKING MASK.)

WHEN WE ALL RETURN TO THE OFFICE, I HOPE MY COLLEAGUES CAN ACCOMMODATE MY 3PM SHOWER SCHEDULE.

REFUSING TO WEAR A MASK IS LIKE REFUSING TO USE A CONDOM.

(ALTHOUGH, I ALMOST SUFFOCATED USING A CONDOM.)

WHEN YOU FART DURING
A ZOOM WORK CALL
AND REALIZE YOUR MIC IS ON,
SO YOU START COUGHING AND
MAKING NOISES WITH YOUR CHAIR
HOPING YOUR TEAM WILL THINK
"MAYBE IT WASN'T A FART?"
AND THEN YOU REALIZE
YOUR CAMERA IS ALSO ON AND
THEY JUST WATCHED YOU
FRANTICALLY WAFTING THE AIR
TO GET RID OF A SMELL THEY
COULD NEVER HAVE DETECTED.

NOW, WHEN WE HOST GUESTS, I MAKE AN EFFORT BY WEARING MY BEST SWEATPANTS.

ZOOM MEETINGS 2020

MAR	"FUNNY" HATS
APR	"FUNNY" BACKGROUNDS
MAY	CAMERA ALWAYS OFF
JUN	"SORRY,
JUL	I
AUG	WAS
SEP	ON
OCT	MUTE."
NOV	DON'T EVEN SAY, "HELLO."
DEC	ZOOM FIST INTO SCREEN

OFFICIAL C.D.C. GUIDELINES

WEAR A MASK IN PUBLIC

OR

TATTOO "DUMBFUCK" ON YOUR FOREHEAD

THE SALON STAMPEDE

HAIR THEY COME...
THE MOPEY MOPHEADS.
THE SHIPWRECK SURVIVORS.
THE FERAL FRO BROS.
THE HAD-A-GO HEROES.
THE MONKS-BY-MISTAKE.
THE SASSY SASQUATCHES.
THE ZOMBIES OF ZOOM.
THE RUBIK'S PUBES.
THE GIBBONS OF GREYSTOKE.
THE NO-SHAVEN HAVENS.
THE BOWL-CUT BEAUTIES.
THE ONE-EARED WARRIORS.
THE CAVEMEN MENTEES.
THE BANGED-UP BANG BANGERS.
THE ROOT TRUTHERS.
THE APE HOUSE APPLICANTS.
THE NECK-HAMSTER HEATHENS.
THE WALKING DEAD ENDS.
THE HAIR-DON'TS OF HAIRDOS.
THE BIG, SOGGY, COUGHED-UP FURBALL OF HUMANITY.

THE POETIC INJUSTICE OF WORKING FROM HOME (2020)

AS THE WORLD AROUND US FELL APART AT THE SEAMS,
WE ALL LOGGED ON TO MICROSOFT TEAMS.

SOME OF US ADDED BACKGROUNDS AND WORE FUNNY HATS,
BUT THE NOVELTY SOON WORE OFF, SO THAT WAS THAT.

WE MADE ELOQUENT STATEMENTS TO END ANY DISPUTE,
ONLY TO REALIZE WE WERE STILL ON MUTE.

NO LONGER FREE-RANGE PEOPLE ABLE TO ROAM,
WE BECAME BATTERY EMPLOYEES CAGED AT HOME.

WE STRUGGLED THROUGH THE WEEK TO GET TO SATURDAY,
BUT FOR MANY, THAT WAS NOW KNOWN AS "SHOWER DAY."

IT WAS HARD TO HAVE A WEEKEND WHEN THE WEEK DIDN'T END,
CONNECTIVITY CAN BE A FOE, AS WELL AS A FRIEND.

WE SUPPORTED EACH OTHER THROUGH OUR NEW WORK LIFE,
THROUGH THICK AND THIN, AND HAIRCUTS BY MY WIFE.

OUR SNACKING STRETCHED STRETCHY PANTS TO A NEW TIME ZONE,
IF YOU LISTENED CAREFULLY, YOU COULD HEAR THE ELASTIC GROAN.

AS HOMESCHOOLING BEGAN, AND OUR KIDS STARTED REMOTE CLASSES,
WE LEARNED ALGEBRA EXISTS TO MAKE US FEEL LIKE DUMBASSES.

BUT WE WERE THERE TO TALK ABOUT THE ELECTION AND BLACK LIVES MATTER,
AND THEY ASKED IMPORTANT QUESTIONS LIKE, "DADDY, ARE YOU GETTING FATTER?"

SO, WHEN WE'RE ALL VACCINATED AND BACK TOGETHER, MY TEAM WILL NOT REFUTE,
THEY'LL FEEL NOSTALGIC, AND LONG FOR THOSE MOMENTS, WHEN I WAS STILL ON MUTE.

YOU ARE NOW VACATING THE QUARANTINE SECTION

YOU'RE PROBABLY VENTURING OUT ON A PERILOUS QUEST TO FIND A TOILET ROLL, PRETENDING TO BE THE STAR OF "INDIANA JONES AND THE LAST CRAP AID." IF SO, BEWARE OF THE GREEDY ASSHOLES AND RAIDERS OF THE LOST SHELVES PANIC-BUYING IN THE WALMART OF DOOM. (BETTER TAKE YOUR BULLWHIP.)

CRAP SUPERHEROES

GLOW-IN-THE-DARK MAN
MR. TIN OPENER
DOCTOR STINKY FINGER
THE HUMAN FERRET
CAPTAIN SHUTTLECOCK
DAN DIARRHEA
THE INCREDIBLE CUNT
SALIVAMAN
THE MARVELOUS MOANER
SUPER SUSAN
THESAURUS THINGY
HALITOSIUS
MACRAMÉ MAN
THE SILVER SPOONER
PROFESSOR LAXATIVE
THE MENOPAUSER
THE SOCIALLY-DISTANCED DUO
THE GROPER
VELCRO-FACE
ORGASMA
CAPTAIN COLD SORE

UBERTY

—Uber for teenagers.

"THAT'S BETTER."

—What your boss says after just making something worse.

IF A SPIDER WALKED ACROSS MY LAPTOP AND TYPED:

"HELLO, MY NAME IS NIGEL. AS A REPRESENTATIVE OF MY SPECIES, I HAVE VOLUNTEERED TO LET YOU KNOW THAT WE MEAN YOU NO..."

(FLICK!)

"SEE YA, NIGEL."

PEACOCK:	"WOW! LOOK AT MY BEAUTIFUL FEATHERS!"
GOD:	"YOU'RE WELCOME."
PEACOCK:	"WHAT ARE THEY FOR?"
GOD:	"FOR ATTRACTING A MATE."
PEACOCK:	"WHAT? SO EVERYONE WILL KNOW WHEN I'M FEELING HORNY?"
GOD:	"WELL, YES, IT'S PART OF YOUR COURTSHIP RITUAL."
PEACOCK:	"CAN'T I DO SOMETHING MORE SUBTLE?"
GOD:	"NO, YOU HAVE TO DISPLAY YOUR PLUMAGE SO THE PEAHEN SEES YOU."
PEACOCK:	"CAN'T YOU JUST GIVE HER BETTER EYESIGHT?"
GOD:	"YOU'RE LUCKIER THAN THE BABOON. HE HAS TO WAVE HIS ERECTION ABOUT."
PEACOCK:	"BABOON? THAT'S A DUMBASS NAME. WHAT AM I CALLED?"
GOD:	"A PEACOCK."
PEACOCK:	"SAY WHAT?"
GOD:	"A PEACOCK."
PEACOCK:	"WHAT THE FUCK? THAT SOUNDS LIKE I HAVE A COCK THE SIZE OF A PEA!"
GOD:	"YES, HENCE THE MAGNIFICENT PLUMAGE."
PEACOCK:	"THE FEATHERS THAT TELL THE WORLD MY TINY COCK IS READY FOR ACTION?"
GOD:	"OH LOOK, HERE COMES A PEAHEN NOW."
PEACOCK:	"OK, FUCK-FEATHERS, LET'S HOPE SHE DOESN'T SUE US FOR FALSE ADVERTISING."

EPITAPH FROM THE STONE AGE

BORN.

TRIED NOT TO GET EATEN BY RAVENOUS BEASTS.

DIED.

EPITAPH FROM THE DIGITAL AGE

BORN.

WORRIED ABOUT DUMB SHIT THAT WASN'T REAL.

DIED.

I ALWAYS EXPECT THE MAXIMUM FROM DOING THE MINIMUM.

ONE DAY, TWEETS WILL
BE SENT WITH JUST
THE POWER OF THOUGHT.

UNTIL THEN,
TWEETS WILL BE POSTED
WITH ZERO THOUGHT.

THE ONLY THING
FUNNIER THAN
A LOUD FART
ON A PACKED TRAIN
IS THE SILENCE
THAT FOLLOWS.

DON'T GET TRAPPED BY YOUR OWN DECISIONS

DUMBASS

PRIZE POSSESSION

—A game show for demons.

SOME PEOPLE LOOK LIKE NATURAL RUNNERS.

I LOOK LIKE I'M FALLING HORIZONTALLY.

WHEN MY FRIEND SAW MY DOG
LICKING ITS DICK AND BALLS
HE SAID,
"I WISH I COULD DO THAT."

I REPLIED,
"GO AHEAD, BUT HE MIGHT BITE YOU."

FAKE IT TILL YOU MAKE IT

WORSE.

YOU RANDOMLY NOD HELLO TO A STRANGER ON THE STREET.

WHEN YOU GET HOME, HE'S STANDING ON YOUR DOORSTEP.

YOU HURRY INSIDE TO FIND HIM SITTING ON YOUR COUCH.

YOU RUN UPSTAIRS TO THE BATHROOM AND LOCK THE DOOR.

WHEN YOU TURN AROUND, HE'S SHITTING ON YOUR TOILET.

—How targeted advertising feels.

ME:
"ARE YOU MAKING A LIST FOR SANTA?"

MY DAUGHTER:
"I'LL SEND YOU THE LINKS."

LIFE ISN'T FAIR

ESPECIALLY WHEN YOU'RE JUDGED BY THE SIZE OF YOUR NIPPLES.

ALAN KEYES

—IKEA Employee of The Month

ANY BIRD THAT DOESN'T FLY AWAY WHEN A HUMAN GETS NEAR MUST HAVE BALLS OF STEEL.

IT'S NOT BRAVE, IT'S TOO HEAVY TO FLY.

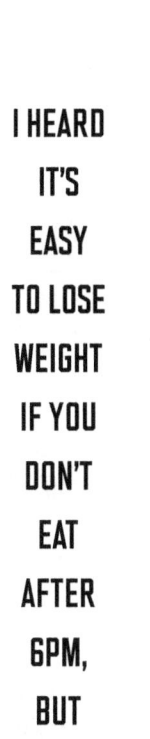

INAPPROPRIATE MOTHER'S DAY CARDS

THANK YOU FOR NOT DRINKING GIN DURING THE FIRST FEW MONTHS OF YOUR PREGNANCY.

THANK YOU FOR YOUR TIRELESS EFFORTS TO WORK WITH DAD'S ERECTILE DYSFUNCTION.

THANK YOU FOR SELFLESSLY ENDING YOUR AFFAIR WITH MY BOYFRIEND.

THANK YOU FOR INTRODUCING ME TO ALL THE GUYS AT THE BAR WHO MIGHT BE MY FATHER.

THANK YOU FOR ALWAYS FAVORING MY YOUNGER, PRETTIER, MORE SUCCESSFUL SISTER TO INSPIRE ME TO BE MORE LIKE HER AND LESS LIKE ME.

JUST ONCE, I'D LIKE SOMEONE TO ARRIVE LATE TO A MEETING AND ANNOUNCE, "SORRY I'M LATE, I WAS DOING A POO."

FAMILY GATHERINGS ARE ALL ABOUT SITTING AROUND THE TABLE TO ENJOY THE DELICIOUS FEUD.

SEND NUDES

TO RUN ERRANDS.

MANHOOD

—A foreskin.

THE PARENTING CODE

MORNING BIRDSONG EASES ME INTO

THE SHALLOW WATERS OF MY SLUMBER.

JUST IN TIME TO HEAR THE LIGHTEST OF LITTLE FEET

CREEPING INTO MY RECEDING DREAM.

MY MIND FLOODS WITH WONDER,

WHICH LITTLE PERSON WILL LAUNCH MY DAY?

CLOSER AND CLOSER I HEAR THE FLOORBOARDS CREAK.

A TINY HAND PATS ME TIMIDLY ON THE SHOULDER.

GENTLE, SWEET BREATH FLOATS AGAINST MY EAR,

AS INQUISITIVE WORDS FROM AN INNOCENT MIND

ARE WHISPERED WITH YOUTH AND PURITY:

"DADDY, WHAT'S THE PASSCODE FOR THE IPAD?"

**BLOWING KISSES AT THE SCHOOL BUS WHEN YOU'RE A DAD:
GOOD.**

**BLOWING KISSES AT THE SCHOOL BUS WHEN YOU'RE NOT A DAD:
BAD.**

FASTPASSHOLES

—People at theme parks who act superior just because they've paid extra.

I GAVE MY WIFE
A T-SHIRT
WITH THE SLOGAN,
"EAGER BEAVER."

SHE APPRECIATED
THE IRONY.

Y

E

T

H

—Using a Ouija Board to ask,
"Is anybody out there?"
and a ghost with a lisp replies.

DOES A BEAR SHIT IN THE WOODS?

YES, WHICH IS WHY YOU'LL NEVER SEE A SQUIRREL WEARING WHITE SNEAKERS.

RELATIONSHIP ETIQUETTE

WHEN DATING: SHOWER THEN SEX

WHEN MARRIED: SEX THEN SHOWER

WHEN LONGTIME MARRIED: SHOWER

WHEN DIVORCED: CASUAL SEX IN SHOWER

WHEN LONGTIME DIVORCED: CHEETOS

IF YOU DON'T GIVE A SHIT,
LIFE GETS SHITTY.

IF YOU GIVE TOO MUCH OF A SHIT,
LIFE GETS SHITTY.

IF YOU JUST GIVE A SHIT,
THAT'S THE SHIT RIGHT THERE.

PIG: "HMM...NO OFFENCE TO YOUR WORK, BUT I'M A BIT UGLY."

GOD: "YES, I HAVE GIVEN YOU A SNOTTY SNOUT, SWEATY-LOOKING SKIN, AND TROTTERS."

PIG: "AND WHAT'S WITH THIS STUPID TAIL?"

GOD: "IT CURLS UP, SO EVERYONE HAS A CLEAR VIEW OF YOUR PUTRID LITTLE RECTUM."

PIG: "WHAT?! CAN'T YOU GIVE ME ANY REDEEMING QUALITIES?"

GOD: "OH, BUT I HAVE...THE FLESH ON YOUR BONES IS ONE OF THE MOST DELICIOUS MEATS ON EARTH."

PIG: "DELICIOUS?"

GOD: "YES, YOUR FLESH CAN TRANSFORM INTO HAM, BACON, GAMMON, AND PORK."

PIG: "THAT SOUNDS LIKE A MENU. I DON'T WANT TO BE A FUCKING MENU!"

GOD: "CALM DOWN. THAT'S WHY I'VE MADE YOU VERY UGLY AND GIVEN YOU THE DESIRE TO LIVE IN MUCK."

PIG: "SO, I HAVE TO COVER MYSELF IN SHIT TO SAVE MY BACON?"

GOD: "EXACTLY. THE OTHER CREATURES, ESPECIALLY HUMANS, MUST NEVER KNOW HOW TASTY YOU ARE."

PIG: "WHY, WHAT'S THE DEAL WITH THESE HUMANS?"

GOD: "LET'S JUST SAY, I HAVE FORSEEN SINFUL ACTS OF MCRIBS AND PORK RINDS."

PIG: "WHAT THE FUCK ARE PORK RINDS?"

GOD: "ALSO KNOWN AS PORK SCRATCHINGS, THEY ARE A SNACK CREATED BY FRYING YOUR SKIN."

PIG: [SILENT]

GOD: [SILENT]

PIG: "OK, LET'S MAKE THIS TAIL EVEN SMALLER, THROW ON SOME NASTY BRISTLES, ADD SOME BAT EARS, AND GET THAT STINKY SHIT READY...THIS LITTLE PIGGY IS BATHING TONIGHT!"

IF YOU CAN SMILE WITH YOUR EYES,

CAN YOU STARE WITH YOUR LIPS?

THE TRUE MAGIC OF DISNEY IS MICKEY NOT LEAVING TURD PELLETS EVERYWHERE LIKE A REAL MOUSE.

I'M JUST TRYING TO GET THROUGH LIFE WITHOUT BECOMING THAT "GOT EATEN BY A WILD ANIMAL" GUY.

THIS REMINDS ME OF YOU...

...A TOTAL WASTE OF SPACE.

I'M SURE MOST OLD PEOPLE LOOK BACK AT THEIR LIVES AND THINK, WHAT THE FUCK WAS THAT SHIT ALL ABOUT?

YOU HAVE TO DO
WHAT YOU DON'T WANT TO DO
TO DO
WHAT YOU DO
WANT TO DO

IF YOU ONLY DO
WHAT YOU WANT TO DO
AND DON'T DO
WHAT YOU DON'T WANT TO DO
YOU'LL BE IN DEEP DOO-DOO

A BIG TURNOFF FOR WOMEN IS MEN WITH BAD GRAMMAR.

SO GENTS, ALWAYS CHECK FOR A PERIOD AND NEVER OVERUSE A COLON.

PLANET EARTH IS A WORLD INHABITED BY A MAJORITY OF KIND AND DECENT HUMAN BEINGS WHO ARE EASILY MANIPULATED BY FEAR-MONGERING AND POLARIZING MEDIA OUTLETS WHO USE THEIR PLATFORMS TO MAKE SURE THE HUMANS VOTE FOR SOCIOPATHIC POWER-HUNGRY LEADERS WHO SUIT THEIR POLITICAL AND GREED-FUELED AGENDAS. THE SCARED YET BRAVE HUMANS ARE THEN ENCOURAGED TO KILL EACH OTHER IN THE NAME OF PATRIOTISM AND RELIGIOUS FAITH, WHILE THE PSYCHOTIC LEADERS AND THE MEDIA MOGULS SIT BACK IN LUXURY LEATHER CHAIRS AND WATCH IT ALL HAPPEN WITH A FINE WHISKEY CARESSING THEIR REPULSIVE EVIL GRINS. THIS MESSAGE WAS BROUGHT TO YOU BY AN OVERPAYING SPONSOR WHOSE C.E.O. DONATED TO A POLITICAL LEADER'S ELECTION CAMPAIGN IN RETURN FOR A POLICY THAT WILL BENEFIT THEIR COMPANY'S PROFITS TO THE DETRIMENT OF HUMANITY AND PLANET EARTH

MEDIEVAL HUMOR

CONDEMNED MAN ON CHOPPING BLOCK:
"PLEASE STOP."

EXECUTIONER:
"I'VE LEARNED TO QUIT WHILE YOU'RE A HEAD."

REMEMBER KIDS,
IF ANYONE SAYS
YOU CAN'T
DO SOMETHING,
OR YOU'RE NOT
GOOD ENOUGH,
THEY'RE
PROBABLY RIGHT,
SO JUST GO
WATCH YOUTUBE.

A SHORT POEM ABOUT PICTURESQUE SCENERY, MURDEROUS INTENT, AND NATURAL ABILITY

IN THE
CATSKILLS,
CATS KILL
WITH
CAT SKILL.

YOU CAN LEAD A HORSE TO WATER, BUT YOU CAN'T MAKE IT USE LESS OF YOUR EXPENSIVE KIEHL'S SHAMPOO.

EVERY TIME MY WIFE LOOKS AT ME, HER FACE LIGHTS UP WITH MILD DISAPPOINTMENT.

Tonight's
Anti-vaxxers'
meeting
has been
canceled
due to illness.

See you next week
(hopefully).

MY NIECE WON A SCHOOL AWARD FOR 100% ATTENDANCE, SO I CONVINCED HER TO SKIP THE AWARD CEREMONY.

THIS IS A TRUE STORY BECAUSE I'M A TOTAL PRICK OF AN UNCLE.

ONLY WHEN YOU ACCEPT WHO YOU ARE, CAN YOU BEGIN TO MOURN WHO YOU'LL NEVER BE.

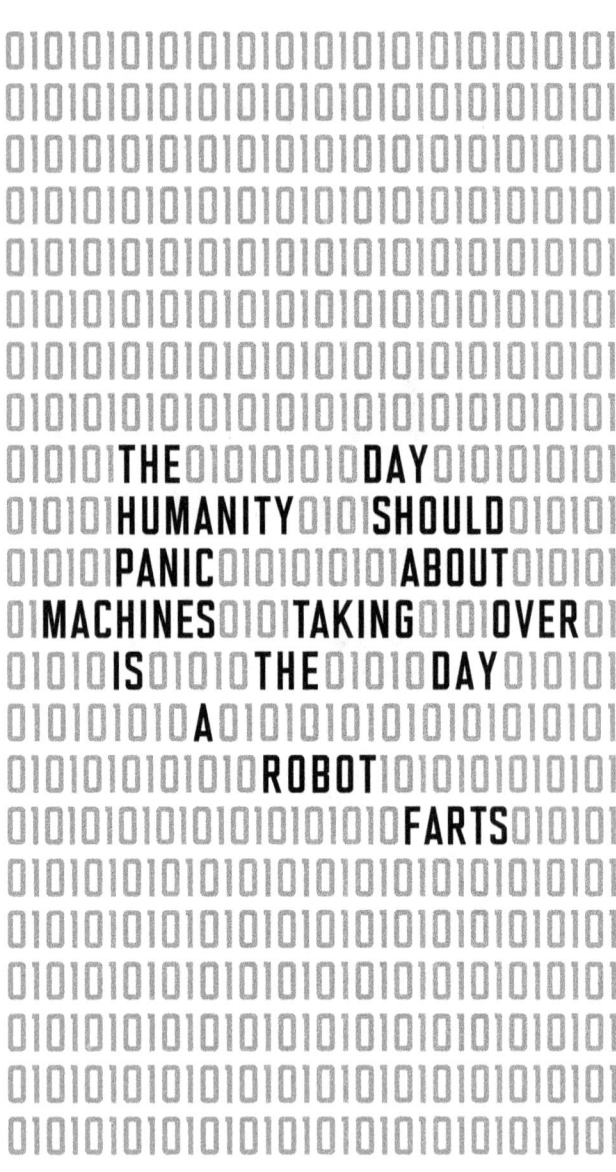

MARRIAGE

—The undying belief
you can change someone
until one of you dies.

I MAY NOT BE THE MOST ATTRACTIVE, TALENTED, OR HARD-WORKING PERSON IN THE WORLD, BUT I'M GREAT AT FAKING HUMILITY.

I USED TO DO A LOT OF SPEED DATING.

NOW I DO A LOT OF SPEED ALONE.

PAT DOWNE

—Airport Security
Employee of The Month

IF ALL OF THE WORLD'S KNOWLEDGE WAS PUT INTO TWO BOOKS:

1. USELESS KNOWLEDGE
2. USEFUL KNOWLEDGE

I'D STILL BE ON BOOK 1.

THE RETURN OF TYLER DURDEN

TYLER DURDEN: "GENTLEMEN, WELCOME TO PUZZLE CLUB. THE FIRST RULE OF PUZZLE CLUB IS, YOU DO NOT TALK ABOUT PUZZLE CLUB. THE SECOND RULE OF PUZZLE CLUB IS, YOU DO NOT TALK ABOUT PUZZLE CLUB. AND THE THIRD AND FINAL RULE, IF THIS IS YOUR FIRST NIGHT AT PUZZLE CLUB, YOU HAVE TO FIGHT."

PUZZLE ENTHUSIAST 1: "FIGHT? WE'RE JUST HERE TO DO JIGSAW PUZZLES."

TYLER DURDEN: "I KNOW, BUT YOU PUZZLE PUSSIES NEED TO LEARN HOW TO FIGHT!"

PUZZLE ENTHUSIAST 2: "WHY?"

TYLER DURDEN: "OH MAN, YOU GUYS ARE JUST LIKE THOSE DUNGEONS AND DRAGONS DICKS."

PUZZLE ENTHUSIAST 3: "CAN WE PUT OUR SHIRTS BACK ON?"

TYLER DURDEN: "FUCK YOU GUYS! I HOPE YOU ALL HAVE A FUCKING PIECE MISSING!"

(TYLER STORMS OUT AND HEADS DOWN THE HALLWAY TOWARDS CHESS CLUB.)

VENN DIAGRAMS EXPLAINED

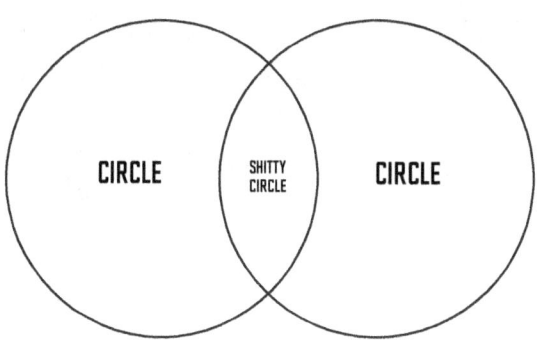

EVERY YEAR, MORE PEOPLE ARE BITTEN BY PEOPLE THAN BY SHARKS.

STAY ON LAND AT YOUR OWN RISK.

"HEAD, SHOULDERS, KNEES AND TOES, KNEES AND TOES."

—Today's specials in a restaurant for cannibals.

SOMEWHERE OUT THERE,
A WOMAN IS BEING
HARASSED BY A
PEST-CONTROL GUY.

CURSING UNNECESSARILY NECESSITATES THERAPY.

FRIEND: "HAVE YOU READ 'THE ART OF SAYING NO'?"

ME: "YES."

FRIEND: "WAS IT GOOD?"

ME: "YEP."

FRIEND: "HAS THE ADVICE CHANGED YOUR LIFE?"

ME: "YEAH."

FRIEND: "CAN I BORROW IT?"

ME: "OF COURSE."

FRIEND: "HAVE YOU READ 'THE POWER OF YES'?"

ME: "NO."

EVERYONE LOVES FATHER'S DAY
UNTIL DAD TAKES ONE OF HIS DAD SHITS.

TRAINED PIGEONS CAN TELL THE DIFFERENCE BETWEEN A PICASSO AND A MONET PAINTING.

WHICH RAISES THE QUESTION...

WHY DID SOMEONE TRAIN PIGEONS TO STUDY ART INSTEAD OF BEING THEIR PERSONAL, BADASS DEATH SQUADRON?

SALADS TAKE SO LONG TO EAT, THEY NEED TO HELP YOU LIVE LONGER TO MAKE UP FOR THE TIME YOU'VE LOST EATING FUCKING SALADS.

CUT THIS OUT.
HANG IT ON YOUR BEDROOM DOOR HANDLE.
INSERT HAMSTER.

WHEN TO SAY "BLESS YOU" AFTER A PERSON SNEEZES

1) WHEN YOU SUSPECT THAT PERSON HAS THE BUBONIC PLAGUE.

2) NO OTHER TIMES.

3) SO, LET'S ALL AGREE TO STOP FUCKING SAYING IT.

ON THE ROAD TO
DAMASCUS,
SAUL BECAME PAUL.

IT DIDN'T
WORK OUT SO WELL
FOR DENIS.

I HATE
DRINKING
ALONE
BECAUSE
I'M SUCH
A BAD
INFLUENCE
ON ME.

LAST NIGHT, I DREAMED I WAS RELAXING ON A STUNNING WHITE SANDY BEACH, SIPPING A REFRESHING COCKTAIL, FEELING THE SUN KISS MY SKIN AS A WARM BREEZE DANCED GENTLY THROUGH MY TOUSLED HAIR. AS I LAY ON MY CUSHIONED LOUNGER, I LOOKED OUT TO THE CALM HORIZON AND CAUGHT A GLIMPSE OF MY TOES, LIGHTLY SUGARED WITH A FEW SOFT GRAINS OF SAND. THEN I REMEMBERED I WAS ON THIS VACATION TO SAY FAREWELL TO MY FEET, BECAUSE FOR A REASON THAT WASN'T CLEAR, WHEN I RETURNED HOME, I HAD TO SAW THEM BOTH OFF. NOT BY A SURGEON UNDER ANESTHESIA, BUT BY ME, IN MY BACKYARD. NOT WITH AN ELECTRIC SAW, BUT ONE OF THOSE HAND SAWS YOU SEE IN OLD CARTOONS. WHEN I AWOKE THIS MORNING, BECAUSE I'M SO RELIEVED IT WAS JUST A DREAM AND I DON'T HAVE TO SAW MY OWN FEET OFF, I FEEL POSITIVE ABOUT MY DAY AHEAD AND HAVE A SPRING IN MY STEP. AND THAT'S JUST ANOTHER EXAMPLE OF HOW MY FUCKED-UP MIND LIKES TO FUCK WITH ME.

IF YOU'RE ALWAYS NICE,
I CAN HANDLE IT.

IF YOU'RE ALWAYS A DICK,
I CAN HANDLE IT.

IT'S THE INCONSISTENCY
THAT FUCKS ME UP.

ABS-URD

—The notion of me ever getting a six-pack.

MANY SUITCASE WARRANTIES DON'T COVER "AN ACT OF GOD."

WHY IS GOD FOCUSED ON DESTROYING YOUR LUGGAGE?

HOW UGLY IS YOUR SUITCASE IF EVEN GOD WANTS TO DESTROY IT?

PERHAPS YOU SHOULD STAY HOME.

SPF 8

MISTER SPIDER,
BASKING IN THE SUN,
YOU REALLY SHOULD PUT
SOME SUNSCREEN ON.
AS I SQUEEZED THE TUBE
TO GET THE DREGS,
HE SAID, "GO ON THEN,
JUST DO MY LEGS."

REJECTED COUNTRY MUSIC SONGS

KISS ME LIKE YOU KISS MAMA.
DON'T COME HOME A JERKIN'.
VEGGIE COWBOY.
PASSIN' GAS GWENDOLINE.
OL' BROKEN DICK'S HONKY TONK WONKY BONK.
LOVE AT FIRST SPITTOON.
A TASSEL FOR EVERY HASSLE.
MAKE LOVE LIKE MY MULE.
CHEATIN' HEARTS, EAT MY FARTS.
GOT SPURS ON MY SNEAKERS.
GRANDMA'S STINKY NIGHTGOWN.
HE SHAVES FOR ME, BUT I DON'T FOR HIM.
GO EASY ON THEM BEANS.
YOU CAN'T KEEP A GOOD HOEDOWN.
PAPA SOILED HIS OL' BLUE JEANS AGAIN.
REDNECKS AND BLUEBALLS.
SUNDAY BEST FOR INCEST.
TAMMY'S TITTIES ARE TEASIN' TEXAS.
SHARTBREAKIN' MAN.
IT ITCHES IN ME BRITCHES.
DON'T MAKE MY BROWN EYE RED.
JESUS TAKE THE WHEEL, BUT DON'T YOU BE A TEXTIN'.

THE IGNORANCE DIET

NO CARBS.

NO SUGAR.

JUST DONUTS.

MY WIFE IS A FART GENIE.

IF I'M ALONE IN A ROOM AND LET OUT A SNEAKY FART...
POOOFFF!
SHE MAGICALLY APPEARS FROM NOWHERE TO GRANT ME HER DISGUST (AND ZERO WISHES).

THIS PAGE IS NOTHING BUT AN ATTENTION SEEKER.

IF IT COULD, IT WOULD BEND OVER AND SHAKE ITS SEXY, TONED ASS CHEEKS.

IT WOULD FLEX ITS RIPPLING ABS WHILE LOUNGING BY AN INFINITY POOL IN PARADISE.

IT WOULD CASUALLY DISPLAY ITS VAPID WEALTH FROM ITS EFFORTLESS SUCCESS.

WE'D "LIKE IT" TO SUSTAIN ITS PSEUDO POWER OVER OUR VULNERABLE MINDS.

WE'D "SHARE IT" TO ESCAPE OURSELVES FOR A SELF-HATING SECOND.

WE'D "POST IT" TO BLINDLY FOCUS ON WHAT WE DON'T HAVE AND IGNORE WHAT WE DO HAVE.

BECAUSE THAT'S OUR ONLY WAY TO GET A MOMENTARY GRASP ON A FAKE EXISTENCE.

SO PITY THIS SAD, DESPERATE LITTLE PAGE.

AND IGNORE YOUR NAIL-BITTEN CHUBBY FINGERS AS YOU TURN TO THE NEXT.

WHAT THE WORLD NEEDS NOW IS ~~LOVE, SWEET LOVE.~~ A MUSICAL PORNO.

EVERY YEAR,
MY NEW YEAR'S
RESOLUTION
IS TO STOP USING
THE "C" WORD.

AFTER ALL,
"COMMITMENT"
IS FOR
DELUSIONAL CUNTS.

I WAS TOLD THERE IS A CURE FOR MASTURBATION, BUT IT WAS JUST LIP SERVICE.

WHEN LIFE WAS SIMPLE

VIKING RECRUITER:
"CAN YOU STAB PEOPLE WITH POINTY THINGS?"

JOB CANDIDATE:
"YES."

VIKING RECRUITER:
"WELCOME ABOARD...YOU START AT DAWN."

"WE NEED TO PUT
A CALENDAR MEETING
ON THE CALENDAR
TO CREATE
MORE CALENDARS,
AND THEN PUT MEETINGS
ABOUT THOSE CALENDARS
ON THE CALENDAR."

—Corporate America

SUSANS AND CAROLS
MUST BE SO RELIEVED
KARENS ARE
TAKING THE HIT.

THE FUTILITY OF SOCIAL MEDIA

SPEND HOURS CREATING A POST.
GET 7 LIKES.
LOOK AT ONE OF THE LIKER'S PROFILES.
SEE THAT "JANET" HAS 19 FOLLOWERS.
START WORKING ON YOUR NEXT POST.

THE ORDINARY CASE OF BARRY BUTTON

—A film about Benjamin Button's brother who's born young and grows older until he dies.

I LOVE EXERCISE.

EVERY DAY,
I EXERCISE MY RIGHT
TO NOT EXERCISE.

ANTI-SOCIAL MEDIA

IF READING TWITTER
ON THE SHITTER
MAKES YOU BITTER
FLUSH THE TYPED LITTER
TO BE MENTALLY FITTER

IF YOU'RE STUPID ENOUGH TO NOT VOTE, THANK YOU FOR NOT VOTING.

STATISTICALLY, CHEERFUL PEOPLE DIE YOUNGER.

(ESPECIALLY ON MONDAYS.)

**EVERY DAY,
I GO FROM
"WHY DON'T I?"
TO
"WHY DIDN'T I?"**

4,837 GNATS:	"WOW, THERE'S A LOT OF US."
GOD:	"YEP."
4,837 GNATS:	"SO, WHAT DO WE DO?"
GOD:	"JUST FLY ABOUT IN A MASSIVE CLOUD TRYING TO MATE WITH EACH OTHER."
4,837 GNATS:	"THAT'S IT?"
GOD:	"NO...IF YOU EVER SEE A PASSING HUMAN, FLY DIRECTLY INTO ONE OF HIS/HER EYEBALLS FOR NO REASON."
4,837 GNATS:	"GOT IT."
GOD:	"I HAVE ALSO ADDED A 'G' TO YOUR NAME THAT'S AS UNNECESSARY AS YOU ARE."

4,837 GNATS ARE NO LONGER LISTENING BECAUSE THEY'RE FRANTICALLY TRYING TO MATE WITH EACH OTHER.
GOD ADMIRES HIS WORK FOR A FEW SECONDS
UNTIL ONE FLIES DIRECTLY INTO HIS LEFT EYEBALL.

IF YOUR KIDS ARE ANNOYING YOU, JUST PUT PHOTOS OF SIMILAR-LOOKING CHILDREN IN A FOLDER TITLED "REPLACEMENT CANDIDATES" AND LEAVE IT ON THE KITCHEN TABLE.

FRIENDSHIP IS MORE IMPORTANT THAN MONEY.

(UNLESS ONE OF THOSE BASTARDS OWES YOU $20 OR MORE.)

AVERAGE GREAT WHITE SHARK:	16 FT.
JAWS:	25 FT.
THE MEG:	75 FT.
JASON STATHAM:	5 FT, 10 IN.
HOLLYWOOD:	GO FUCK YOURSELF.

LIFE IS
SOMEONE IN YOUR FUCKING WAY.

MEN ONLY FART WHEN THEY EAT, DRINK, OR DO NEITHER.

IF YOU DON'T KNOW YOUR LIMITATIONS, THEY QUICKLY BECOME OBVIOUS TO EVERYONE ELSE.

ME:
"I'M DOING NO-BEER BECEMBER."

FRIEND:
"BECEMBER DOESN'T EXIST."

ME:
"EXACTLY."

SOMETIMES, I WONDER IF I'M JUST A SECRET EXPERIMENT GOING WRONG, AND SOON A PISSED OFF SCIENTIST WILL PAY HIS GLOATING COLLEAGUE $100 BECAUSE HE LOST THE BET.

IF YOU THINK YOUR LIFE IS SHIT,

IMAGINE BEING A FLIGHTLESS BIRD.

AN ACTUAL NEWS HEADLINE

SPIDER BITES AUSTRALIAN MAN ON PENIS AGAIN.

AGAIN?

WAS IT THE SAME SPIDER?

IS THERE A PENIS-PROTECTION COURSE THIS MAN COULD TAKE?

IS THIS THE SUPERHERO ORIGIN STORY WE'VE ALL BEEN WAITING FOR?

IS THERE A NEW SPECIES OF COCK-MUNCHING ARACHNID WE SHOULD KNOW ABOUT?

SERIOUSLY, IS THERE?

MY SPIDEY SHAFT IS TINGLING.

SCIENTISTS CLAIM SMILING CAN LENGTHEN YOUR LIFE.

UNLESS THAT SMILE BELONGS TO A SERIAL KILLER.

(OR AN AUSTRALIAN DICK-DEVOURING SPIDER.)

"RESISTANCE IS FUTILE."

—What I whisper to my pants at Thanksgiving.

EVERY TIME I GO TO IKEA WITH MY WIFE,
WE SPEND SO MUCH TIME IN THERE,
I START TO BELIEVE,
"THIS IS WHERE WE LIVE NOW."

WIFE:

"WHY DOES THE DOG BARK AT ME WHEN I'M IN THE SHOWER?"

HUSBAND:

"BECAUSE HE THINKS YOU'RE PLAYING WITH A CHIPMUNK."

SUPPORTING IDEAS YOU DON'T SUPPORT.

—Welcome to middle management.

"GRANDE ESPRESSO FOR TODD."

—If God ordered at Starbucks.

IF YOU STARE AT SOMEONE'S EARS LONG ENOUGH, THEY LOOK FAKE AND STUCK ON.

(TRY IT IN YOUR NEXT MEETING.)

YESTERDAY, I MET A GUY WHO SAID HE'S "BORN AGAIN."

HIS MOM MUST BE EXTREMELY ACCOMMODATING.

I DON'T BELIEVE IN CONFIRMATION BIAS.

IN FACT, EVERY ARTICLE I'VE READ DOESN'T BELIEVE IN IT EITHER.

ME:
"YOU CAN'T AVOID HEARING SWEAR WORDS ON THE STREET, BUT THAT DOESN'T MEAN YOU SHOULD USE THEM."

MY 9-YEAR-OLD SON:
"LIKE WHEN THAT LADY ON HER PHONE SAID, 'SUCK MY MOTHERFUCKING DICK'?"

ME:
"YES, THAT WAS WRONG."

MY 9-YEAR-OLD SON:
"I KNOW. SHE DOESN'T HAVE A DICK."

**PETTING ZOO:
GOOD.**

**HEAVY-PETTING ZOO:
BAD.**

TO PROVE ROMANCE IS NOT DEAD, LIGHT A FEW CANDLES AND SCATTER ROSE PETALS BEFORE YOU WHACK OFF LIKE A RABID GIBBON WRESTLING WITH AN ENRAGED MOLLUSK.

KKKunts

—Enough said.

WAITER:
"ANY ALLERGIES?"

ME:
"SMALL PORTIONS."

IMAGINE YOU'RE SUFFERING FROM ACID REFLUX, SO A DOCTOR PUTS AN ENDOSCOPE DOWN YOUR THROAT AND FINDS THE CAUSE TO BE AN ANGRY, MINIATURE VERSION OF YOU WHO MUST HAVE BEEN THERE SINCE YOU WERE BORN. SO YOU GO INTO SURGERY TO HAVE "LITTLE YOU" REMOVED, BUT DURING THE PROCEDURE, YOU DIE AND "LITTLE YOU" LIVES. THEN "LITTLE YOU" BEGINS TO LIVE YOUR LIFE AND WRITES A BESTSELLING MEMOIR ABOUT BEING TRAPPED IN A LIVING HELL (WHICH WAS YOU) AND GETS RICH FROM A SUBSEQUENT MOVIE DEAL. ONE DAY, "LITTLE YOU" STARTS TO SUFFER FROM ACID REFLUX, SO "LITTLE YOU" SIMPLY DRINKS SOME PEPTO-BISMOL (WHICH INSTANTLY CURES IT) AND GOES ON TO LIVE A LONG, FRUITFUL, AND HAPPY LIFE.

SOME GUYS EXERCISE TO COMPETE IN IRONMAN TRIATHLONS.

I EXERCISE TO STOP MY NIPPLES POINTING AT THE FLOOR.

BIRTH [▭▭▭▭▭▭▭▭▭▭▭▭▭▭▭   ] DEATH

NOW LOADING: "STRESS"
TIME REMAINING: ?

QUANTITTIES

—Large breasts

MY DRY JANUARY ALWAYS BECOMES CLOUDY WITH MANY DAMP SPELLS.

WHEN SOMEONE SAYS,
"DANGER IS MY MIDDLE NAME,"
THEY'RE ALSO SAYING,
"ANNOYING IS MY FIRST NAME
AND CUNT IS MY SURNAME."

THE OLDER YOU GET, THE MORE YOUR BIRTHDAY SUIT NEEDS IRONING.

THAT "JOLLY RANCHER" IS PRETTY HAPPY FOR A MAN WHO CAN'T POSSIBLY HAVE ANY TEETH LEFT.

MY WIFE LONGED TO HEAR THE PATTER OF TINY FEET, SO I CANCELED OUR PEST-CONTROL SERVICE.

IF YOU EVER QUESTION THE FUTILITY OF LIFE, JUST GOOGLE "CHICKEN WEARING JEANS."

THIS PAGE WAS BROUGHT TO YOU BY THE LATEST DENIM COLLECTION FROM VICTORIA PECKHAM.

COMPANY POLICY #278C

WE REFUSE TO JUDGE EACH OTHER NEGATIVELY.

IF WE DID, WE WOULD ALL BE EXHAUSTED.

LAST NIGHT, I DREAMED THAT POLICE CAUTION TAPE WAS EDIBLE AND DELICIOUS.

I THEN BEGAN HUNTING FOR CRIME SCENES SO I COULD ENJOY A SNACK.

NOW I'M AWAKE, EATING A BOWL OF BLAND CORNFLAKES, WONDERING, "WHAT IF?"

PLEASE SPARE A THOUGHT FOR ALL OF THE INCONTINENT PLUMBERS OUT THERE.

LOVE ALWAYS FINDS A WAY

TO FUCK UP YOUR DAY.

EVERYONE IS OVERCOMPENSATING FOR A LACK OF SOMETHING.

FITNESS COMMERCIALS:
"DO YOU HAVE STUBBORN BELLY FAT?"

ME:
"YES, BUT MINE IS ALSO RUDE, SARCASTIC, AND SOCIALLY AWKWARD."

G.G.O.A.T.

—Greatest Goat Of All Time

A PROOFREADER
ONCE USED
"SUPERHEROES"
TO SAVE ME
FROM HAVING
"SUPERHERPES".

THE PRIMARY PURPOSE
OF A LIFE JACKET ON
A PLANE IS TO
HELP THE AUTHORITIES
LOCATE YOUR
LIFELESS BODY GENTLY
BOBBING ON THE WAVES.

Welcome to Necrophiliacs Anonymous.

Please leave your shovels by the door, and help yourself to a breath mint.

**AT WHAT AGE SHOULD
WE STOP EXPECTING
A HIGH-FIVE FOR
CLEANING OUR TEETH?**

WHY IS IT SO EASY TO LAUGH AT AN OLD MAN'S TESTICLES?

THEY'RE
LOW
H
A
N
G
I
N
G
FRUIT

THE ANATOMY OF A PUPPY

HE WHO QUOTES POETRY,
IS A PRETENTIOUS TWAT,
WHO NEEDS A FALLING TREE,
ON HIS HEAD TO GO SPLAT.

OR A REAL TREAT TO SEE,
FOR POETIC HEAVEN,
A CRAZED SQUIRREL IN A TREE,
WITH AN AK-47.

ON A POSITIVE NOTE,
YOUR BIGGEST REGRET
IS YET TO COME.

GET YOUR FUCKING EYES TESTED.

DON'T START BELIEVIN'.

IF YOU'VE ENJOYED READING THIS BOOK AS MUCH AS I'VE ENJOYED WRITING IT, ALL I CAN DO IS APOLOGIZE AND HOPE YOU'RE ABOUT TO DO SOMETHING MORE FUN, LIKE A STARING CONTEST WITH AN ANGRY SPIDER, PLAYING TWISTER WITH AN AMPUTEE SUPPORT GROUP, OR EVEN AN ILLEGAL BARE-KNUCKLE FIGHT WITH A BEAR (WHO SHAVED HIS PAWS TO QUALIFY). WHATEVER IT IS, MAKE SURE YOU DO IT WITH A TOUCH OF HUMANITY AND A FUCKING SHITLOAD OF PROFANITY.

NO ANIMALS WERE HARMED DURING THE MAKING OF THIS BOOK.

BUT IF YOU SEE A WASP, PLEASE USE IT TO SMACK THE LIVING FUCK OUT OF THAT EVIL LITTLE FUCKFACE FUCKER.

AND IF IT'S A MURDER HORNET, DON'T STOP HITTING UNTIL THAT BITCH IS DUST.

AND IF IT'S A SWARM OF MURDER HORNETS, BUY AN ARSENAL OF BOOKS, RECRUIT AN ARMY, AND GET OUT THERE SWINGING, SOLDIER! YOUR COUNTRY NEEDS YOU.

ACKNOWLEDGEMENTS

THANK YOU TO MY EXTREMELY PATIENT QUARANTEAM:

MY WIFE AND PERSONAL HAIR-HACKER, MAIJA.

MY GREY-HAIR-INDUCING CHILDREN, LIV AND LUKE.

AND MY HAIRBRAINED DOG, LEO THE LUNATIC,
WHO WILL SOON BE GETTING NEUTERED
(A PAINFUL METAPHOR FOR EVERY MAN'S LIFE).

WITHOUT YOU ALL, I WOULD BE A LOT WEALTHIER.

www.ingramcontent.com/pod-product-compliance
Lightning Source LLC
Chambersburg PA
CBHW070527090426
42735CB00013B/2895